TOUCHSTONE

STUDENT'S BOOK 4B

MICHAEL McCARTHY
JEANNE McCARTEN
HELEN SANDIFORD

CAMBRIDGE
UNIVERSITY PRESS

CAMBRIDGE
UNIVERSITY PRESS & ASSESSMENT

Shaftesbury Road, Cambridge CB2 8EA, United Kingdom

One Liberty Plaza, 20th Floor, New York, NY 10006, USA

477 Williamstown Road, Port Melbourne, VIC 3207, Australia

314–321, 3rd Floor, Plot 3, Splendor Forum, Jasola District Centre, New Delhi – 110025, India

103 Penang Road, #05–06/07, Visioncrest Commercial, Singapore 238467

Cambridge University Press & Assessment is a department of the University of Cambridge.

We share the University's mission to contribute to society through the pursuit of education, learning and research at the highest international levels of excellence.

www.cambridge.org
Information on this title: www.cambridge.org/9781107637481

First published 2005
Second Edition 2014

20 19 18 17 16 15 14 13 12 11

Printed in Mexico by Litográfica Ingramex, S.A. de C.V.

A catalogue record for this publication is available from the British Library

ISBN 978-1-107-68043-2 Student's Book
ISBN 978-1-107-62430-6 Student's Book A
ISBN 978-1-107-63748-1 Student's Book B
ISBN 978-1-107-68275-7 Workbook
ISBN 978-1-107-62708-6 Workbook A
ISBN 978-1-107-69602-0 Workbook B
ISBN 978-1-107-66153-2 Full Contact
ISBN 978-1-107-67936-8 Full Contact A
ISBN 978-1-107-66763-1 Full Contact B
ISBN 978-1-107-68151-4 Teacher's Edition with Assessment Audio CD/CD-ROM
ISBN 978-1-107-61272-3 Class Audio CDs (4)

Additional resources for this publication at www.cambridge.org/touchstone2

Acknowledgments

Touchstone Second Edition has benefited from extensive development research. The authors and publishers would like to extend their thanks to the following reviewers and consultants for their valuable insights and suggestions:

Ana Lúcia da Costa Maia de Almeida and Mônica da Costa Monteiro de Souza from **IBEU**, Rio de Janeiro, Brazil; Andreza Cristiane Melo do Lago from **Magic English School,** Manaus, Brazil; Magaly Mendes Lemos from **ICBEU**, São José dos Campos, Brazil; Maria Lucia Zaorob, São Paulo, Brazil; Patricia McKay Aronis from **CEL LEP**, São Paulo, Brazil; Carlos Gontow, São Paulo, Brazil; Christiane Augusto Gomes da Silva from **Colégio Visconde de Porto Seguro,** São Paulo, Brazil; Silvana Fontana from **Lord's Idiomas**, São Paulo, Brazil; Alexander Fabiano Morishigue from **Speed Up Idiomas**, Jales, Brazil; Elisabeth Blom from **Casa Thomas Jefferson**, Brasília, Brazil; Michelle Dear from **International Academy of English**, Toronto, ON, Canada; Walter Duarte Marin, Laura Hurtado Portela, Jorge Quiroga, and Ricardo Suarez, from **Centro Colombo Americano**, Bogotá, Colombia; Jhon Jairo Castaneda Macias from **Praxis English Academy**, Bucaramanga, Colombia; Gloria Liliana Moreno Vizcaino from **Universidad Santo Tomas**, Bogotá, Colombia; Elizabeth Ortiz from **Copol English Institute (COPEI),** Guayaquil, Ecuador; Henry Foster from **Kyoto Tachibana University,** Kyoto, Japan; Steven Kirk from **Tokyo University**, Tokyo, Japan; J. Lake from **Fukuoka Woman's University**, Fukuoka, Japan; Etsuko Yoshida from **Mie University**, Mie, Japan; B. Bricklin Zeff from **Hokkai Gakuen University**, Hokkaido, Japan; Ziad Abu-Hamatteh from **Al-Balqa' Applied University**, Al-Salt, Jordan; Roxana Pérez Flores from **Universidad Autonoma de Coahuila Language Center**, Saltillo, Mexico; Kim Alejandro Soriano Jimenez from **Universidad Politecnica de Altamira**, Altamira, Mexico; Tere Calderon Rosas from **Universidad Autonoma Metropolitana Campus Iztapalapa**, Mexico City, Mexico; Lilia Bondareva, Polina Ermakova, and Elena Frumina, from **National Research Technical University MISiS**, Moscow, Russia; Dianne C. Ellis from **Kyung Hee University**, Gyeonggi-do, South Korea; Jason M. Ham and Victoria Jo from **Institute of Foreign Language Education, Catholic University of Korea**, Gyeonggi-do, South Korea; Shaun Manning from **Hankuk University of Foreign Studies**, Seoul, South Korea; Natalie Renton from **Busan National University of Education**, Busan, South Korea; Chris Soutter from **Busan University of Foreign Studies**, Busan, South Korea; Andrew Cook from **Dong A University**, Busan, South Korea; Raymond Wowk from **Daejin University**, Gyeonggi-do, South Korea; Ming-Hui Hsieh and Jessie Huang from **National Central University**, Zhongli, Taiwan; Kim Phillips from **Chinese Culture University**, Taipei, Taiwan; Alex Shih from **China University of Technology,** Taipei Ta-Liao Township, Taiwan; Porntip Bodeepongse from **Thaksin University**, Songkhla, Thailand; Nattaya Puakpong and Pannathon Sangarun from **Suranaree University of Technology**, Nakhon Ratchasima, Thailand; Barbara Richards, Gloria Stewner-Manzanares, and Caroline Thompson, from **Montgomery College**, Rockville, MD, USA; Kerry Vrabel from **Gateway Community College**, Phoenix, AZ, USA.

Touchstone Second Edition authors and publishers would also like to thank the following individuals and institutions who have provided excellent feedback and support on _Touchstone Blended:_

Gordon Lewis, Vice President, Laureate Languages and Chris Johnson, Director, Laureate English Programs, Latin America from **Laureate International Universities; Universidad de las Americas**, Santiago, Chile; **University of Victoria**, Paris, France; **Universidad Technólogica Centroamericana**, Honduras; **Instititut Universitaire de Casablanca**, Morocco; **Universidad Peruana de Ciencias Aplicadas**, Lima, Peru; **CIBERTEC**, Peru; **National Research Technical University (MiSIS)**, Moscow, Russia; **Institut Obert de Catalunya (IOC),** Barcelona, Spain; Sedat Çilingir, Burcu Tezcan, and Didem Mutçalıoğlu from **İstanbul Bilgi Üniversitesi,** Istanbul, Turkey.

Touchstone Second Edition authors and publishers would also like to thank the following contributors to _Touchstone Second Edition:_

Sue Aldcorn, Frances Amrani, Deborah Gordon, Lisa Hutchins, Nancy Jordan, Steven Kirk, Genevieve Kocienda, Linda-Marie Koza, Geraldine Mark, Julianna Nielsen, Kathryn O'Dell, Nicola Prentis, Ellen Shaw, Kristin Sherman, Luis Silva Susa, Mary Vaughn, Kerry S. Vrabel, Shari Young, and Eric Zuarino.

Authors' Acknowledgments

The authors would like to thank all the Cambridge University Press staff and freelancers who were involved in the creation of *Touchstone Second Edition*. In addition, they would like to acknowledge a huge debt of gratitude that they owe to two people: Mary Vaughn, for her role in creating *Touchstone First Edition* and for being a constant source of wisdom ever since, and Bryan Fletcher, who also had the vision that has led to the success of *Touchstone Blended Learning*.

Helen Sandiford would like to thank her family for their love and support, especially her husband Bryan.

The author team would also like to thank each other, for the joy of working together, sharing the same professional dedication, and for the mutual support and friendship.

Finally, the authors would like to thank our dear friend Alejandro Martinez, Global Training Manager, who sadly passed away in 2012. He is greatly missed by all who had the pleasure to work with him. Alex was a huge supporter of *Touchstone* and everyone is deeply grateful to him for his contribution to its success.

Touchstone Level 4B Contents and learning outcomes

Interaction	Skills				Self study
Conversation strategies	**Listening**	**Reading**	**Writing**	**Free talk**	**Vocabulary notebook**
• Speak informally in "shorter sentences" • Use expressions like *Uh-oh!* and *Oops!* when something goes wrong	***Wedding on a budget*** • Listen to people plan a wedding; check what they agree on and what they'll do themselves ***Fix it!*** • Match conversations with pictures; then check which problems were solved	***Developing your problem-solving skills*** • An article about an interesting problem-solving technique	***A good solution*** • Write a proposal presenting a solution to a problem at work • Format for presenting a problem and its solution	***Who gets help with something?*** • Class activity: Ask and answer questions to find out who gets help	***Damaged goods*** • Find out if new words have different forms that can express the same idea, and use them in sentences
• Use expressions such as *That reminds me (of) . . .* to share experiences • Use *like* informally in conversation	***Similar experiences*** • Listen to two people share experiences, and number the incidents in order; then answer questions ***Good and bad apologies*** • Listen to conversations; match the people to the apologies; then decide if they were effective	***Apologies: The key to maintaining friendship*** • An article about the importance of apologizing and suggesting ways to do so	***A note of apology*** • Write an email apologizing for something • Expressions for writing a note of apology	***How did you react?*** • Group work: Tell a story about an incident, and listen and respond to classmates' stories	***People watching*** • Learn new vocabulary by making a connection with something or someone you know, and write true sentences
• Report the content of conversations you have had • Quote other people or other sources of information	***Who's materialistic?*** • Listen to someone answer questions, and take notes; then report his answers ***I couldn't live without . . .*** • Listen to four people talk about things they couldn't live without, and complete a chart; then listen and write responses to opinions	***This Stuff's Gotta Go!*** • A blog post about a woman who declutters her home	***I couldn't live without . . .*** • Write an article about your classmates and things they feel they couldn't live without • Use of reporting verbs for direct speech and reported speech	***Material things*** • Pair work: Ask and answer questions about material things	***Get rich!*** • When you learn a new word, notice its collocations – the words that are used with it
Checkpoint Units 7–9 pages 95–96					
• Use tag questions to soften advice and give encouragement • Answer difficult questions with expressions like *It's hard to say*	***Great advice*** • Listen to a conversation and answer questions ***Success is . . .*** • Listen to four conversations about success, and complete a chart	***Three Child Stars Who Beat the Odds*** • A magazine article about actors who have managed to avoid "Child Star Syndrome"	***A success story*** • Write a paragraph about someone you know who has achieved success, and explain why that person became successful • Topic and supporting sentences in a paragraph	***Quotations*** • Group work: Define success	***Do your best!*** • Learn new idioms by writing example sentences that explain or clarify meaning
• Refer back to points made earlier in a conversation • Use more formal vague expressions like *and so forth* and *etc.*	***Trends in the workplace*** • Listen to conversations about trends, and identify advantages and disadvantages ***Trends in technology*** • Listen to four people talk about trends, and write notes on their views	***The Internet – The new pathway to success?*** • An article about the recent trend of using the Internet to become successful	***Trends in technology*** • Write a comment on a web article about trends in technology • Expressions for describing trends	***What's trending?*** • Group work: Discuss trends	***Try to explain it!*** • Write definitions in your own words to help you learn the meaning of new words and expressions
• Introduce what you say with expressions like *The best part was (that) . . .* • Use *I don't know if . . .* to introduce a statement and involve the other person in the topic	***An interesting job*** • Listen to a personal trainer talk about her job; write notes ***A fabulous opportunity!*** • Complete a job ad, and listen to check and answer questions	***Ace that Interview!*** • An article about how to answer the most common questions in job interviews	***A fabulous opportunity!*** • Write a cover letter in response to an ad • Format for writing a cover letter for a job application	***The best person for the job*** • Group work: Interview the members of your group for a job	***From accountant to zoologist*** • When you learn a new word, learn other words with the same root as well as common collocations to expand your vocabulary quickly
Checkpoint Units 10–12 pages 127–128					

Useful language for . . .

Working in groups

We're ready now, aren't we?

Are we ready? Let's get started.

Haven't I interviewed you already?

I've already interviewed you, haven't I?

Where are we?

We're on number ________.

We haven't quite finished yet.

Neither have we.

We still need more time – just a few more minutes.

So do we.

One interesting thing we found out was that ____________.

________ told us that ____________.

Checking with the teacher

Would it be all right if I missed our class tomorrow? I have to ________.

I'm sorry I missed the last class. What do I need to do to catch up?

When are we supposed to hand in our homework?

Excuse me. My homework needs to be checked.

I'm sorry. I haven't finished my homework. I was going to do it last night, but ________.

Will we be reviewing this before the next test?

"________" means "________," doesn't it? It's a regular verb, isn't it?

I'm not sure I understand what we're supposed to do. Could you explain the activity again, please?

Could I please be excused? I'll be right back.

UNIT 7

Problem solving

Can Do! In this unit, you learn how to . . .

Lesson A
- Talk about things others do for you using *get* and *have*

Lesson B
- Describe household problems using *need* + passive infinitive or *need* + verb + *-ing*

Lesson C
- Speak informally in "shorter sentences"
- Use expressions like *Uh-oh* and *Ouch* when things go wrong

Lesson D
- Read an article about problem solving
- Write a proposal on how to solve a problem

Before you begin . . .

Where do you go when . . .

- you need a haircut?
- you need new glasses?
- you need some photocopies?
- there's a big stain on your jacket?
- you need a memory card for your camera?
- your car or motorcycle breaks down?

Lesson A Getting things done

Do it yourself!

We asked people what jobs they do themselves in order to save money. Here's what they said:

Have you ever cut your own hair to save money?

"I have, actually. But it looked so bad that I went to the most expensive place in town and had a hairdresser cut it again. I'll never try that again! Now I always get it cut professionally at a good hair salon, though I get a friend to cut my bangs occasionally. That saves me some money."

—Min-sook Kim, Seoul, South Korea

Do you do your own car repairs?

"Well, I can do routine things like put oil in the car. But, to be honest, I get my brother to fix most things. And if there's something seriously wrong with my car, I have my uncle take a look at it at his garage. I can get it fixed there pretty cheaply. I also have it serviced there once a year."

—Marcus Aldóvar, Bogotá, Colombia

Do you do your own home decorating?

"My wife and I are having a new house built right now, but we're going to do all the painting and decorating ourselves. We've done it before. My sister's an interior designer, so we'll have her choose the colors and get her to pick out curtains, too. She's got great taste."

—Martin and Jill Snow
Calgary, Canada

Do you ever do your own repairs around the house?

"Not anymore! Once I tried fixing the dishwasher myself because I didn't want to pay to have someone come and repair it. But I didn't realize I had to turn off the water first. So I fixed the problem, but I flooded the entire apartment! And it cost a fortune to have the water damage repaired."

—Bella Clark, Miami, U.S.A.

1 Getting started

A **Which of these things do you do yourself? What other jobs do you do? Make a class list.**

cut your own hair	do your own repairs around the house	put oil in your car
decorate your home	fix your computer	

B 3.01 **Listen. What jobs have the people above done themselves? Were they successful?**

Figure it out **C** **Complete *b* so it has a similar meaning to *a*. Use the interviews to help you.**

1. a. I ask my brother to fix things. b. I ________ my brother ________ things.
2. a. We'll ask my sister to choose the colors. b. We'll ________ my sister ________ the colors.
3. a. Someone in a salon cuts my hair. b. I ________ my hair ________ at a good salon.
4. a. I had to pay someone to repair the damage. b. I had to ________ the damage ________ .

2 Grammar Causative *get* and *have* 3.02

Extra practice p. 146

You can use *get* and *have* to talk about asking other people to do things for you.

When you want to show who you ask, you can use *get* + *someone* + *to* + verb or *have* + *someone* + verb.

I **get my brother to fix** my car.
We'll **get my sister to choose** colors for our house.
My hair looked bad, so I **had a hairdresser cut** it again.
I didn't pay to **have someone repair** my dishwasher.

When who you ask is not important, use *get* or *have* + *something* + past participle.

I **get my car fixed** at my uncle's garage.
I always **get my hair cut** professionally.
We're **having a new house built** now.
It cost a lot to **have the water damage repaired**.

About you **A** **Circle the correct options, and write your own answers to the questions. Then ask and answer the questions with a partner.**

1. Do you usually get your hair (cut) / **to cut** professionally? How often do you get it cut?
   I always get my hair cut professionally. I usually . . .
2. Have you ever **had / gotten** a friend cut your hair? How did it turn out?
3. Do you have a bicycle, motorcycle, or car? Where do you get it **fixed / fix**?
4. If you had a flat tire, would you get someone **to change / change** it for you or do it yourself?
5. Do you ever take clothes to the dry cleaner's? Is it expensive to get things **to clean / cleaned**?
6. Do you iron your own clothes? Do you ever get someone **iron / to iron** things for you?
7. Do you ever fix things around the house, or do you have small jobs **done / do** by a professional?

B **Pair work** **What things do people often have done professionally? Make a list. Then discuss each item on your list. Where do you get them done? Is it expensive?**

"Well, people often get their cars cleaned professionally. We get a local company to clean ours."

3 Listening Wedding on a budget

A 3.03 **Listen to Molly and Mark talk about things they need to do to get ready for their wedding. What topics do they agree on? Check (✓) the boxes.**

1

2

3

4

5

6

B 3.03 **Listen again. Which things are Molly and Mark going to have done professionally? Which things are they or their families going to do themselves? Make two lists.**

About you **C** **Pair work** **Imagine you are organizing a wedding or a family event. What things would you do? What would you have someone else do?**

"If I had to organize a wedding, I'd get my friends to take the photos."

Lesson B What needs to be done?

1 Building language

A 3.04 **Listen. What is Isaac good at fixing? Practice the conversation.**

Anna Isaac, something's wrong with the shower. It won't turn off completely. It keeps dripping.

Isaac Yeah? Maybe the showerhead needs replacing.

Anna Oh, it's probably just a washer or something that needs to be replaced. Can you take a look at it?

Isaac Me? I'm not a plumber. I don't even know what's wrong with it.

Anna I know. But you're always so good when the TV needs to be fixed. You know, when the screen needs adjusting.

Isaac Yeah, well, that's an emergency!

Figure it out **B** **Find two different ways to say *We need to replace the showerhead* in the conversation. Complete the sentences below.**

The showerhead needs ____________ . **OR** The showerhead needs ____________ .

2 Grammar *need* + passive infinitive and *need* + verb + *-ing* 3.05

Extra practice p. 146

You can use *need* to talk about things that should be done.

***need* + passive infinitive**	***need* + verb + *-ing***
The TV needs **to be fixed**.	The TV needs **fixing**.
The screen needs **to be adjusted**.	The screen needs **adjusting**.

The structure *need* + verb + *-ing* is mainly used for everyday chores like fixing, changing, cleaning, adjusting, replacing, recharging, etc.

Common errors

Don't use *I need* + verb + *-ing* to say what you are going to do.

*I **need to change** my tire.*
(NOT *I need ~~changing~~ my tire.*)

A **Complete the sentences below in two ways. Use *need* + passive infinitive and *need* + verb + *-ing*. Compare with a partner.**

1. My computer's very slow. Maybe the memory *needs to be upgraded / needs upgrading* (upgrade).
2. There's a problem with our car. The brakes ____________ (adjust).
3. I can't make any calls right now because my cell phone ____________ (recharge).
4. My camera is always going dead. The batteries ____________ (replace) constantly.
5. The closet light won't turn on. The bulb ____________ (change or tighten).
6. Our air conditioner isn't working very well. Maybe the filter ____________ (clean).
7. One of our bookshelves is falling apart. It ____________ (fix).
8. There are bills and papers all over the house. They ____________ (file).
9. Our piano is out of tune. It really ____________ (tune).

About you **B** **Pair work Are any of the sentences above true for you? Do you have any similar problems?**

A I don't have any problems with my computer, but some software needs to be upgraded.

B Yeah? My keyboard needs replacing. Some of the keys aren't working properly.

3 Building vocabulary

A Anna is pointing out more problems to Isaac. Can you guess the things she's talking about? Complete the sentences below. Then compare answers with a partner.

1. "The *microwave* **isn't working**. Nothing's happening. It **won't turn on**."
2. "The ______________ **is leaking**. And there's **a dent** in the door."
3. "The ______________ **keeps flickering** on and off. And I **got a shock** from it."
4. "The ______________ is **loose**. If it **falls off**, we won't be able to open the door."
5. "The ceiling ______________ **is making a funny noise**."
6. "The ______________ has **a** big **scratch** on it."
7. "That ______________ is **torn**. And look – there's **a** big **hole** in the other one."
8. "There's **a** coffee **stain** on the ______________."
9. "The ______________ is a half hour **slow**. Actually, it **stopped**. The battery must be **dead**."

Word sort **B** Can you think of two items for each of the problems below? Do you have any things like these that need to be fixed? Tell a partner.

Things that often . . .	Things that are often . . .	Things that often have . . .
leak: *refrigerator, pen*	scratched:	a dent in them:
fall off:	torn:	a stain on them:
make a funny noise:	loose:	a hole in them:
won't turn on:	slow:	dead batteries:

Vocabulary notebook p. 74

C **Pair work** Make a "to do" list for Anna and Isaac, and prioritize each task. How can they get the problems fixed? Which things need to be done right away?

A They need to get their microwave fixed. They should get someone to look at it.

B Actually, I think it probably needs to be replaced.

You OK?

1 Conversation strategy Speaking in "shorter sentences"

A What kinds of jobs do you get your friends to help you with? Make a class list.

B 3.06 Listen. What are Kayla and Hector trying to do? Do they succeed?

Kayla Hi, there. . . . Ooh! Want some help?
Hector Sure. Just take that end. Got it?
Kayla Yeah. Think so. Oops! Wait a second.
Hector OK. . . . Ready? One, two, three, lift.
Kayla Ooh, it's heavy! . . . Ow! Just broke a nail.
Hector Ouch! You OK?
Kayla Yeah. But hurry up!
Hector There. Shoot! It's not straight.
Kayla Want me to fix it? . . . Better?
Hector Yeah, . . . up a bit on the left.
Kayla There you go. Done.
Hector Thanks. Like it?
Kayla Love it. It looks good. Really good.
Hector Want some coffee?
Kayla No, thanks. Can't drink it. Got any soda?
Hector Sure. . . . Uh-oh! Don't have any. Sorry.

C **Notice** **how Kayla and Hector speak in "shorter sentences." They leave out words like *I* or *you* and verbs like *do*, *be*, and *have*. People often do this in informal conversations, especially when it's clear who or what they're talking about. Find more examples.**

"(Do you) Want some help?"
"(I) Just broke a nail."
"(Are) You OK?"

D Rewrite the conversation with shorter sentences. Compare with a partner and practice.

A Do you need this screwdriver? Here it is.
B Thanks. I can't get this shelf off the wall.
A Do you want me to try getting it off for you?
B Yes, thanks. Are you sure you've got time?
A Yes. . . . OK. That's done. Do you need help with anything else?
B Thank you. No, there's nothing else. Would you like a drink?
A I'd love one. Have you got any green tea?

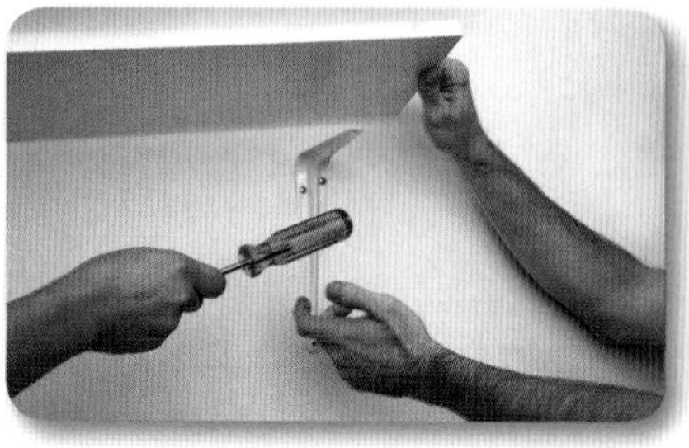

2 Strategy plus *Uh-oh!*

You can use words like *Uh-oh!* and *Oops!* when something goes wrong.

Ooh!	=	when you see a problem
Uh-oh!	=	when you suddenly discover a problem
Oops! / Whoops!	=	when you make a small mistake
Ow! / Ouch!	=	"That hurt." / "It sounds like that hurt."
Shoot!	=	"Oh, no!" (a general reaction)
Ugh! / Yuck!	=	"It's disgusting."

Write an expression you can use in each situation. Can you think of more expressions you can use? Compare with a partner.

1. You drop a hammer on your toe. *Ow!*
2. You miss an important phone call. ______
3. You spill coffee on the table. ______
4. A friend tells you how she broke her arm. ______
5. You realized you just missed a class. ______
6. You put too much sugar in your coffee. ______

3 Speaking naturally Short question and statement intonation

Questions: *Ready?* *OK?* **Statements:** *Ready.* *OK.*

A 3.07 **Listen and repeat the words above. Notice the rising intonation for short questions and falling intonation for short statements.**

B 3.08 **Listen. Is each sentence a question or a statement? Add a question mark (?) or a period (.).**

1. Better *?*
2. Got it ____
3. Broke a nail ____
4. Left a bit ____
5. Done ____
6. You need help ____
7. Got a drink ____
8. Ready ____

4 Listening and strategies Fix it!

A 3.09 **Listen to four people talk about things they are trying to fix. Number the pictures 1 to 4. There is one extra picture.**

☐ ______

☐ ______

☐ ______

☐ ______

☐ ______

B 3.09 **Listen again. Do they solve the problems? Write *Yes* or *No* on the lines.**

C Pair work **Choose one of the pictures, and write a conversation using shorter sentences. Perform it to another pair. Can they guess what activity you are doing?**

A You OK? Need some help?
B Yeah. This just fell off. Can't get it back on.

Sounds right p. 138

Thinking outside the box

1 Reading

A **What's the best way to solve problems? Do you do any of these things? Tell the class.**

- ☐ Ignore the problem and do something else.
- ☐ Brainstorm or make a mind map.
- ☐ Watch your favorite comedy before you start.
- ☐ Try different solutions until one works.
- ☐ Concentrate on the problem in a quiet place.
- ☐ Take enough time to think of ideas.

B **Read the article. Which of the ideas above are recommended?**

Reading tip

As you read, highlight two or three useful collocations you can use in your daily life, such as *tackle an assignment*, *solve a problem*.

DEVELOPING YOUR PROBLEM-SOLVING SKILLS

Can you solve these two classic puzzles?

1. **You have a candle and a box of thumbtacks. How can you attach the candle to the wall?**
2. **Two ropes hang from the ceiling. They're too far apart for you to hold both ropes at the same time. They need to be tied together. How can you tie them?**

Daily life presents us with a huge variety of problems, many of which seem to have no ready or easy solutions. From deciding which apartment to rent to figuring out how to tackle an assignment at school or work, or even handling relationships, day in and day out we have to find ways of solving our problems. Techniques like brainstorming, mind mapping, or listing the pros and cons of different options take an analytical approach and involve "left-brain" thinking. While these techniques can be successful and lead to solutions, good problem solvers tend to switch between this analytical (left-brain) thinking and a more creative and emotional (right-brain) approach.

However, recent research into the brain's behavior while problem solving suggests that traditional techniques for solving problems — concentrating on a task and focusing on finding a solution — may not be the most effective after all. What might be more significant is simply inspiration — that sudden "aha" moment when the solution to a problem appears.

Neuroscientist Mark Beeman's studies into brain activity show that inspiration happens in the brain's right temporal lobe — an area that *isn't* associated with concentration at all. It's an area of the brain that's responsible for facial recognition, connecting memories, and understanding language. Brain imaging scans show a constant low frequency activity in this area, indicating that it's always quietly working in the background of our minds. Beeman suggests that when you're *not* focused on a particular task, for example when you're relaxing before bed or taking a walk, the constant brain "chatter" quiets and the temporal lobe can make connections between distant, unrelated memories. Less than two seconds before inspiration hits, there's a burst of high frequency activity, and eureka! You have a solution.

Now that scientists know *where* problem solving happens, they're beginning to understand *how* to improve it. In tests, people solved more puzzles after watching funny videos than after watching boring or scary movies. This is probably because the people who were watching the funny videos were more relaxed, thus allowing the temporal lobe to perform more effectively.

People were also more likely to solve the puzzles in an "aha!" moment than by analysis. Beeman suggests this is because when people are happy, their brains notice a wider range of information.

The conclusion seems to be that if you want to solve a problem, don't focus on it. Let your brain be quiet and the answer might arrive in a sudden flash of inspiration. Now try solving the problems in the box again. Aha – did it work?

ANSWERS:
1. Tack the box to the wall and stand the candle on top.
2. Attach something heavy to one of the ropes and swing it toward the other.

C **Are the statements below true or false according to the article? Check (✓) the boxes.**

	True	False
1. Good problem solvers use the right side of their brain more than the left.	☐	☐
2. The right temporal lobe is active all the time.	☐	☐
3. When the brain is busy, it makes faster connections between memories.	☐	☐
4. Watching videos makes it more difficult for people to solve problems.	☐	☐
5. When people are in a good mood, they are more able to solve problems.	☐	☐

D **Read the article again. Answer the questions. Then discuss with a partner.**

1. What does the latest research say about the traditional techniques for problem solving?
2. What are three things that happen in the brain's right temporal lobe?
3. How does brain activity change in the moments before you find a solution to a problem?
4. What kind of videos should you watch to improve your problem-solving ability?
5. What *shouldn't* you do if you want to make inspiration more likely to arrive?

2 Speaking and writing A good solution

A **Group work Read the problem below. Discuss your ideas and agree on a solution.**

The events management company that you work for is holding a Movie Awards Ceremony in your city five days from now. Famous actors and directors are attending as well as the international media. However, you have just received very bad news. A serious fire has completely destroyed the concert hall where the event is supposed to be. The Awards Committee wants to cancel the event, but you will lose millions of dollars, and the city is depending on the awards to boost its tourism industry. What can you do to save your event?

B **Read the proposal below. Then write your own proposal persuading the Awards Committee to agree to your ideas. Describe the problem and how you plan to solve it.**

Home | Edit | Document Elements | Tables | Table Layout | Charts | Smart Art

Proposal for a venue alternative

The fire at the concert hall means it is impossible to hold the Movie Awards there next week. Cancelling the event would result in losses of millions of dollars in advertising and ticket refunds.

We could solve this problem by using an alternative venue near the city. The venue is smaller, but we propose to show the ceremony on big screens outside. This would benefit the event in several ways. First of all, people who don't have tickets could also watch it. . . .

Changing venues will mean a lot of reorganization in a short time. We have several plans to make this possible. A local company will provide the screens in exchange for free advertising . . .

Help note

Presenting a solution

- Present and explain the problem.
- Offer a solution and explain its benefits.
- Explain how the solution will be implemented.

C **Read your classmates' proposals. What are the best ideas?**

Free talk p. 132

Vocabulary notebook Damaged goods

Learning tip *Different forms of the same word*

When you learn a new word, find out what type of word it is – a verb, a noun, an adjective, etc. – and whether it has a different form that can express the same idea.

There's a <u>leak</u> in the bathroom. (noun)	*There's a <u>scratch</u> on this DVD. (noun)*
The pipe <u>is leaking</u>. (verb)	*This DVD <u>is scratched</u>. (adjective)*

1 What's wrong with Mark's things? Complete the two sentences for each problem. Use the words in the box.

dent / dented   leak / leaking   scratch / scratched   stain / stained   tear / torn

1. There's a big ________ in the wheel of Mark's mountain bike. It's ________ .
2. There's a dark ________ on his T-shirt. It's ________ .
3. His shorts are ________ . There's a ________ in them.
4. His sunglasses are ________ . They have a ________ on them.
5. There's a ________ in his water bottle. It's ________ .

2 Word builder Find out the meaning of the underlined words below. Then rewrite the sentences using a different form of the underlined word.

1. My coffee mug is <u>chipped</u>.
2. The mirror is <u>cracked</u>.
3. There's a lot of <u>rust</u> on my car.
4. There's a lot of <u>mold</u> in my shower.

On your own

Look around your home. What problems are there? Label each one. Remove the label when the problem is fixed!

Can Do! Now I can . . .

✓ I can . . .   ? I need to review how to . . .

- ☐ talk about things you have other people do for you.
- ☐ talk about things that need to be fixed.
- ☐ use short sentences in informal conversations.
- ☐ use expressions like *Uh-oh* when something goes wrong.
- ☐ understand a conversation about planning an event.
- ☐ understand people talking about things they need to fix.
- ☐ read an article about problem-solving skills.
- ☐ write a proposal presenting a solution to a problem.

UNIT 8

Behavior

Can Do! In this unit, you learn how to . . .

Lesson A
- Talk hypothetically about the past using *would have*, *should have*, and *could have*

Lesson B
- Describe emotions and personal qualities
- Speculate about the past using *must have*, *may have*, *might have*, and *could have*

Lesson C
- Share experiences using expressions like *That reminds me (of)*
- Use *like* in conversation

Lesson D
- Read an article on making apologies
- Write a note of apology

1

2

3

4

Before you begin . . .

Can you think of any situations that would make you . . .

- hug someone?
- laugh out loud?
- sulk? mope?
- lose your temper?
- hang up on someone?
- get mad and yell at someone?

Lesson A Reactions

Last night this guy called, trying to sell me something. Normally, I would have been more polite – you know, I would have just said no and then hung up. But he was the fourth caller in three hours, and it was after 10:00. So I just lost it. I yelled at him for several minutes, and I finally hung up on him. At that point, I couldn't have done much else, I don't think, because I was too mad. I know I shouldn't have lost my temper – he was just doing his job – but, I mean, what would you have done? Would you have gotten mad? I suppose I could have apologized. Or I could have asked him to put me on their "do not call" list. Actually, that's what I should have done. I'll do that next time!

1 Getting started

A **What kinds of unwanted calls do people get? If you get unwanted calls, what do you say?**

"Well, I get calls from people who are trying to sell things. I usually say . . . "

B 3.10 **Listen to Amelia tell her friends about a phone call she got last night. What made Amelia lose her temper? How did she behave toward the caller?**

Figure it out **C** **What does Amelia say about her behavior? What do you think? Complete the sentences. Then compare with a partner.**

Amelia says . . .

1. I shouldn't ______________________.
2. I could ______________________.
3. What would you ______________________?

I think . . .

4. Amelia shouldn't ______________________.
5. I would ______________________.
6. I wouldn't ______________________.

2 Speaking naturally Reduction of *have* in past modals

Amelia should ***have*** *been more polite. (should****'ve****)*
She shouldn't ***have*** *lost her temper. (shouldn't****'ve****)*
She could ***have*** *apologized. (could****'ve****)*
She couldn't ***have*** *done much else. (couldn't****'ve****)*
I would ***have*** *said no and hung up. (would****'ve****)*
I wouldn't ***have*** *yelled at him. (wouldn't****'ve****)*

A 3.11 **Listen and repeat the sentences. Notice the reduction of *have*.**

About you **B** **Pair work** **Which sentences do you agree with? Tell a partner.**

A Amelia really should have been more polite.
B I agree. She shouldn't have lost her temper.

3 Grammar Past modals 3.12

Extra practice p. 147

You can use *would / should / could* + *have* + past participle to talk hypothetically about the past.

Imagine your behavior in a situation:	What **would** you **have done**? I **would have said** no politely. I **wouldn't have lost** my temper.	**Would** you **have gotten** mad? Yes, I probably **would have.**
Say what was the right thing to do:	What **should** she **have done**? She **should have said** no politely. She **shouldn't have yelled** at him.	**Should** she **have yelled** at him? No, she really **shouldn't have.**
Say what other possibilities there were:	What else **could** she **have done**? She **could have told** him not to call again. She **couldn't have done** much else.	**Could** she **have been** more polite? I feel she **could have.**

In conversation

I would is 20 times more common than *I'd* with past modals.

About you **A Read the situations and complete the questions. Then write your own answers. How many ideas can you think of?**

1. Josh saw someone in a parked car throw litter out of the window. He picked it up and threw it right back into the car. Should he *have thrown* (throw) it back in? What else could he ______________ (do)?
   He shouldn't have thrown it back in the car. He could have . . .
2. Sofia was late for a meeting because she slept late. She called the office and told them she'd gotten tied up in traffic. What other excuses could she ______________ (make)? Should she ______________ (tell) the truth?
3. Dan was in a parking lot. He saw a driver accidentally hit another car. The driver left thinking that no one had seen him. What could Dan ______________ (say)? What should the driver ______________ (do)?
4. Katy saw her boyfriend talking to another girl. She called him, told him she didn't want to see him again, and then hung up. Should she ______________ (hang) up? How else could she ______________ (react)?
5. Andrea's friends were making too much noise late one night. Her father yelled at them and asked them to leave. Should he ______________ (lose) his temper? How else could he ______________ (respond)?
6. Jun was in a café. A girl pushed past him and spilled his coffee on him. She just walked away. Could she ______________ (offer) to clean it up? Should she ______________ (apologize)?

B Pair work Compare your ideas and discuss the situations above. What would you have done?

"Actually, I don't think I would have done anything. I would have been annoyed, but . . ."

4 Talk about it True stories

Group work Take turns telling true stories about the situations below. Listen to your classmates and make suggestions. How should they have reacted? What could they have done differently?

Think about the last time you . . .

- weren't very polite.
- had an argument.
- hung up on someone.
- lost your temper.
- sulked or moped.
- made a complaint.

Lesson B Emotional intelligence

1 Building vocabulary

A **Read the article. Do you agree or disagree with the statements? Check (✓) the boxes.**

EMOTIONAL INTELLIGENCE

Emotional ***intelligence*** is the ability to manage your own and other people's emotions. Emotionally **intelligent** people can express their feelings clearly and appropriately, and they are generally optimistic and positive, with high self-esteem. Take the quiz and find out if you have high EQ. (Answer below.)

	AGREE	DISAGREE
SELF-AWARENESS		
1. I'm **decisive**. I know what I want.	☐	☐
2. I'm not **impulsive**. I think before I act.	☐	☐
3. **Jealousy** is not part of my life. I am not a **jealous** person.	☐	☐
MANAGING EMOTIONS		
4. I don't feel **guilty** or **ashamed** about things I've done in the past.	☐	☐
5. **Aggressive** people don't **upset** me. I can cope with their **aggression**.	☐	☐
6. I don't get **angry** and **upset** if people disagree with me.	☐	☐
MOTIVATION		
7. I'm very **motivated**, and I set **realistic** goals for myself.	☐	☐
8. I have the **confidence**, **determination**, and **self-discipline** to achieve my goals.	☐	☐
9. My main **motivation** in life is to make others **happy**.	☐	☐
EMPATHY		
10. I know when my friends feel **sad** or **depressed**.	☐	☐
11. I'm very **sympathetic** when a friend has a problem.	☐	☐
12. I think it's important to be **sensitive** to how other people are feeling.	☐	☐
SOCIAL SKILLS		
13. If friends want to do things I don't want to do, I try to be **flexible**.	☐	☐
14. I think it's good to express emotions like **grief**, **hate**, and **anger**, but in private.	☐	☐
15. **Honesty** is important to me. I'm **honest** with people unless it will upset them.	☐	☐

People with good EQ would agree with the statements above. The more Agree answers you gave, the higher your EQ score.

About you **B** **Pair work Compare your answers. Are you alike? Give more information.**

"I'm usually pretty decisive. It doesn't take me long to make decisions."

Word sort **C** **Complete the chart with nouns and adjectives from the article. Then choose five words from the chart, and make true sentences about people you know to tell a partner.**

noun	adjective	noun	adjective	noun	adjective
aggression	*aggressive*	guilt		realism	
	angry	happiness		sadness	
	confident	honesty			self-disciplined
depression			intelligent	sensitivity	
	determined	jealousy		shame	
flexibility			motivated	sympathy	

Vocabulary notebook p. 84

2 Building language

A 3.13 Listen. What guesses do Paul and Ella make about why their friends are late?

Paul So, where are Alexis and Sam? Do you think they might have forgotten?

Ella They couldn't have forgotten. I talked to Alexis just yesterday. They must have gotten tied up in traffic.

Paul Or they might have had another one of their fights. Maybe Sam is off somewhere sulking, like the last time.

Ella Either way, Alexis would have called us on her cell phone.

Paul Well, she may not have remembered to take it with her. She forgets things when she's stressed out.

Ella That's true. . . . Oh, guess what? My phone's dead! So she could have tried to call and not gotten through.

Paul Oh, my gosh! The movie's about to start. We'd better go in.

Figure it out **B Can you think of some reasons why Alexis and Sam are late? Complete the sentences below. Use the conversation to help you.**

1. They must ____________.
2. They could ____________.
3. They may ____________.

3 Grammar Past modals for speculation 3.14

Extra practice p. 147

You can use *must* / *could* / *may* / *might* + *have* + past participle to speculate about the past.

They **must have gotten** tied up in traffic. = *I'm sure they got tied up in traffic.*
She **could have tried** to call. = *It's possible she tried to call.*
They **may** / **might have had** a fight. = *Maybe they had a fight.*
She **may not** / **might not have remembered**. = *It's possible she didn't remember.*

Use *could not* + *have* + past participle to say what is not possible.

They **couldn't have forgotten.** = *It's not possible they forgot.*

In conversation

Affirmative statements with past modals are much more common than negative statements.

A Imagine these situations. Complete the two possible explanations for each one.

1. One of your co-workers hasn't shown up for a meeting.
   She may ____________ (forget), or she could ____________ (get) tied up in another meeting.
2. You've sent your friend several text messages. She hasn't replied.
   She must ____________ (not / receive) my messages. Her phone might ____________ (die).
3. A friend promised to return a book he borrowed. He hasn't. He's normally very reliable.
   He could ____________ (lose) it. On the other hand, he might ____________ (not / finish) it yet.
4. A friend walked past you in the street and didn't stop to talk. She looked upset.
   She could ____________ (not / see) you. She must ____________ (have) something on her mind.
5. Your brother is supposed to drive you to the airport. He's already 20 minutes late.
   His car must ____________ (break) down. Or he may ____________ (not / remember).

Common errors

Use the past participle, not the base form of the verb.

*They could have **tried** to call.*
(NOT *They ~~could have try~~ to call.*)

B Pair work **Think of two other explanations for each situation above. Discuss the possibilities.**

Sounds right p. 138

I had that happen to me.

1 Conversation strategy Sharing experiences

A Think of different ways to complete this sentence. Tell the class.

I get upset when people ____________ on the subway.

B 3.15 Listen. What annoys Mara and Hal?

Mara Hey! That guy almost knocked you over getting off the elevator.

Hal Yeah. He acted like we were in his way.

Mara I get so annoyed with people like that.

Hal Me too. Like, I get upset when people push on the subway. It's so rude.

Mara Yeah, and speaking of rude people, how about the people who stand right in front of the subway doors and won't let you get off?

Hal Oh, I had that happen to me just last night. These guys were like totally blocking the doors. And when I tried to get past them, they were like, "What's your problem?"

Mara That reminds me of the time I got on the subway with my grandfather, and all these people pushed ahead of him to get seats.

Hal Isn't he like 80 years old?

Mara Yeah. I probably should have said something, but I didn't.

C Notice how Mara and Hal use expressions like these to share their experiences. Find examples in the conversation.

I had that happen to me.
That happened to me.
I had a similar experience.
That reminds me (of) . . .
That's like . . .
Speaking of . . . ,

D Match the comments and responses. Then practice with a partner.

1. I hate it when you're going to park your car and someone takes your parking spot. _____
2. We went to this restaurant once. The waiter got our orders all wrong. He was terrible. _____
3. Don't you hate it when people start texting in the middle of a movie at the theater? _____
4. I was in line at an ATM last week, and this guy cut in line – he walked right in front of me. It was so rude. _____

a. Yeah. That's like when people are talking, and you miss something. It's so annoying.
b. I had that happen to me. This woman almost hit my car. I should have said something to her.
c. Speaking of rude people, I had a similar experience in the bank today. Someone pushed ahead of me.
d. That happened to me, so I complained. The manager just said sorry. We should have gotten a free dessert, at least!

About you **E Pair work** **Do you agree with the people above? Have you had similar experiences? Discuss.**

"I had that happen to me. Someone took my parking spot. They nearly hit my car."

2 Strategy plus *like*

You can use *like* . . .

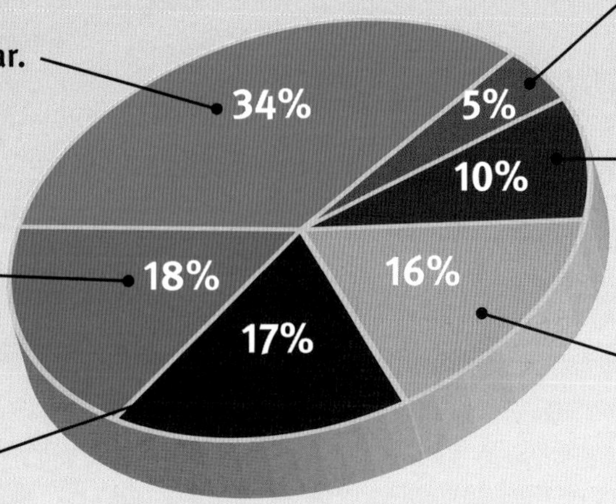

To say something is similar. *He acted like we were in his way.*

To highlight something.* *They were like totally blocking the doors.*

To mean other things, including the verb *like*.

To say "approximately."* *Isn't he like 80 years old?*

To report what someone said.* *They were like, "What's your problem?"*

To give an example. *Like, I get upset . . .*

*Use in very informal conversations only.

In conversation

Like is one of the top 15 words. It is about six times more frequent in conversation than in writing.

3.16 **Read the comment below. Use *like* to replace the underlined words, and add other words you need. Then listen and check your answers.**

"One of my friends is kind of sensitive. ~~For example~~ *Like*, she thinks I'm criticizing her all the time when I'm just – how can I say this? – ________ trying to make a suggestion. She says, ________, "Stop telling me what to do all the time." I guess I'm just more decisive than she is. I know I annoy her sometimes, but otherwise we get along really well. I guess we've been friends for about ________ ten years. It's funny. In other ways we're just the same as ________ each other."

3 Listening and strategies Similar experiences

A 3.17 **Listen to two people talk about their experiences with taxicabs. Number the incidents 1 to 5 in the order that they talk about them.**

- ☐ The cab driver wanted a tip.
- ☐ The cab driver scratched another vehicle.
- ☐ The cab driver nearly caused an accident.
- ☐ The cab driver got lost.
- ☐ The cab driver was having an argument on his phone.

B 3.17 **Listen again. Complete the sentences. Then answer the questions.**

1. The woman says, "I had a similar experience ________________." What happened?
2. The man says, "That reminds me of the time I was taking a cab home ________________." Why did the cab driver make rude comments?
3. The man says, "That's like when they ________________." What example does he give?
4. The woman says, "I had that happen to me. The taxicab ________________." What happened?

About you **C Pair work Have you had any similar experiences with taxicabs? Discuss with a partner.**

Free talk p. 133

1 Reading

A Think of a time when you apologized to someone. How did you do it? What advice do you have for someone making an apology? Make a list of "dos and don'ts."

"Don't wait too long." *"Make sure your apology is sincere."*

B Read the article. Does the writer have any of the same advice?

APOLOGIES: THE KEY TO MAINTAINING FRIENDSHIPS

It's not always convenient or easy to say you're sorry. Sometimes we're too preoccupied to notice when we've hurt someone, or if we do, too busy to make a proper apology. In other cases, personal pride keeps us from admitting we've done something wrong. There are probably times when deep down we feel that we weren't entirely at fault, that the other person owes us an apology! Nevertheless, if we want to maintain good relationships with friends and colleagues, it's essential to know when and how to apologize:

1. ______________________ Even if it feels awkward to say you're sorry, do it as soon as possible. If you wait for the perfect moment, you may end up not apologizing at all. At the same time, if you've waited a bit too long, remember that it's never too late to say you're sorry and set things right.

2. ______________________ Don't let your personal pride get in the way of apologizing. Accept fully that you might have said or done something hurtful. Don't say, "I'm sorry if I offended anyone" or "I'm sorry you feel that way." This implies that you didn't really do anything wrong, that the other person is just overly sensitive. None of us is perfect, and there's no reason to feel embarrassed about needing to apologize.

3. ______________________ Our mistakes often have unpleasant consequences. An apology isn't complete unless you take responsibility both for hurting someone's feelings and for the specific problems you may have caused in that person's life.

4. ______________________ To show you're sincerely sorry, offer to repair any damage you've done. If you've broken something, offer to replace it. If you forgot a birthday, offer to take your friend out to dinner. Or if you're not sure what to do, say, "How can I make this up to you?"

5. ______________________ After admitting that you made a mistake, promise not to do it again, and keep to your commitment! If you have to apologize over and over for the same offenses, you'll soon lose the confidence of your friends.

Finally, sometimes we hesitate to say we're sorry because we feel the other person is more at fault and should apologize first! In these cases, remember that there are rights and wrongs on both sides of any conflict. Even if what happened wasn't 100 percent your fault, be the first to come forward and offer an apology. This act of kindness will make it clear just how much you value the other person's friendship. And it will make you feel better, too.

C Write the missing subheadings in the article.

a. Offer to make things right.
b. Apologize right away.
c. Promise to act differently in the future.
d. Acknowledge any damage caused.
e. Admit you did something wrong.

Reading tip

Read the subheadings in an article first to see what it covers.

D **Find expressions in the article that are similar to the underlined expressions in the questions. Then ask and answer the questions with a partner.**

1. Do you ever get so busy thinking about something that you forget to do things?
2. Have you ever said you were sorry, but secretly in your mind didn't mean it?
3. Can you think of any situations where it feels really uncomfortable to apologize?
4. What kinds of things keep people from apologizing?
5. Have you ever said to anyone, "How can I compensate for this?" What had you done?

2 Speaking and listening Good and bad apologies

A 3.18 **Listen to four conversations. Why is each person apologizing? Match the person to the reason. Write the letter. There is one extra reason.**

1. Alex ____
2. Nora ____
3. Gregory ____
4. Adriana ____

a. forgot to meet a friend.
b. handed in an assignment late.
c. forgot someone's birthday.
d. offended a friend.
e. got into an argument.

B 3.18 **Listen again. Were the apologies effective? Give reasons. Complete the chart.**

	Was it effective?	Why or why not?
1. Alex	Yes / No	____
2. Nora	Yes / No	____
3. Gregory	Yes / No	____
4. Adriana	Yes / No	____

About you **C** **Pair work** **How would you apologize in the situations above? Discuss your ideas.**

3 Writing A note of apology

A **Read the email and the Help note. Underline the expressions Jason uses to apologize. Does his email follow the advice from the article on page 82?**

To: angiebrown@cup.org
From: jason978@cup.org

Dear Angela,

I just wanted to say that I'm truly sorry for getting into an argument with John at your party last night. The argument was totally my fault. You warned me before the party that I shouldn't discuss politics with him, and I did it anyway! I could see that you were very upset, and I feel really terrible about it. I promise never to get into an argument at your house again, and I will always listen to your advice in the future. I just hope that you can forgive me for this.

Sincerely,
Jason

Help note

Writing a note of apology

I just wanted to say I'm sorry for (not) ____ ing . . .
I would like to apologize for . . .
I feel I should apologize for . . .
I promise not to ____ again.
It was my fault entirely.

About you **B** **Think of a time when you apologized or should have apologized to someone. Write an email to apologize. Then read your classmates' emails. Are the apologies effective?**

Vocabulary notebook / People watching

Learning tip *Making connections*

When you learn new vocabulary, make a connection with something or someone you know. Think of how or when you would use the word or expression to talk about your life.

In conversation

Happy talk

People say ***happy*** more than they say ***sad*** or ***unhappy***.

happy
sad
unhappy

1 Think of a person you know for each of the qualities below.

1. _________ has a lot of self-confidence.
2. _________ is very good at controlling his or her anger.
3. _________ has no sympathy for people who complain a lot.
4. _________ has the motivation and determination to do well at work.

2 Write a sentence for each adjective. Make a connection with a person or an experience.

aggressive	flexible	impulsive	sensitive
depressed	guilty	jealous	

My sister says she feels guilty when she eats too much chocolate.

3 Word builder Find and write the meaning of these expressions. Use words in Unit 8 to help you.

1. be / feel down in the dumps _____________
2. be full of yourself _____________
3. be / turn green with envy _____________
4. be heartless _____________
5. be set on doing something _____________
6. go nuts / bananas _____________

On your own

Do some people watching! The next time you are out and about, watch the people around you. Write notes when you get home.

Can Do! Now I can . . .

✓ I can . . . ? I need to review how to . . .

- ☐ talk about reactions and behavior.
- ☐ talk hypothetically about the past.
- ☐ describe emotions and personal qualities.
- ☐ speculate about the past.
- ☐ use expressions like *That reminds me (of)* to share experiences.
- ☐ use *like* in informal conversations.
- ☐ understand people sharing taxi experiences.
- ☐ understand a conversation about rude behavior.
- ☐ read an article on making apologies.
- ☐ write a note of apology.

UNIT 9

Material world

Can Do! In this unit, you learn how to . . .

Lesson A
- Talk about possessions and being materialistic
- Report things that people said

Lesson B
- Discuss money management
- Report questions that people asked

Lesson C
- Report the content of conversations
- Quote other people or sources of information

Lesson D
- Read a blog about decluttering
- Write a survey article about your classmates' possessions

1

2

3

4

Before you begin . . .

- What are your most important possessions?
- Is having a lot of possessions a good thing or bad thing?
- Do you think you are materialistic?

BUT IS IT ART?

British artist destroys his possessions.

"My goal is to destroy all my possessions. I have been making an inventory of everything I own, and it comes to 7,006 items, from televisions to reading material to records to old love letters to my Saab 900. These are the things I have accumulated in the 37 years of my life. Some of them are hard to part with, like my father's sheepskin coat, which he gave to me many years ago. But I have made a conceptual decision as an artist to shred and granulate everything."

". . . I am also destroying artwork – my own as well as some by my friends. They said it was OK. They understand my project. At the end of this week, after my possessions are turned into granules, I want to bury them underground in a shopping center. I haven't found the right shopping center yet."

A conveyor belt takes Michael Landy's possessions to a shredding machine.

1 Getting started

A **What kind of art do you see around your town or city? Make a list. Do you like it?**

"You see a lot of sculptures in the park. Some are interesting."

B **Read what artist Michael Landy says about one of his projects. What is the project? Could you do the same thing with all your possessions?**

C **3.19 Listen to Ginny talk about the article. Which facts didn't she get right? Do you agree with her opinion?**

"I read about this British artist who came up with a really unusual art project. He said his goal was to destroy all his possessions and that he wanted to bury them in a parking lot! Can you believe it? He explained that he had been making a list of everything he owned and that it came to 17,000 items! And that he had made an artistic decision to shred and granulate everything. You can actually watch him destroying all his things. Someone explained to me that this is 'performance art.' I guess this guy really hates materialism. So do I, but I can't throw anything away. Just the same, maybe I'll stop buying so much stuff. . . . You know, I wonder why he didn't just give his stuff away. But I think it's a really interesting idea. I'd like to know more about this type of art."

Figure it out **D** **Complete these sentences to report what Michael Landy said. Use Ginny's interview to help you.**

1. Landy said his goal ____________ to destroy all his possessions.
2. He explained some things ____________ hard to part with.
3. He said his inventory ____________ to 7,006 items.
4. He said he ____________ a decision to bury them, but he ____________ the right place yet.

2 Grammar Reported speech 3.20

Extra practice p. 148

When you report the things people said, the verb tense often "shifts back."

Direct speech	**Reported speech**
Michael Landy:	He said (that) . . .
"My goal **is** to destroy all my possessions."	his goal **was** to destroy all his possessions.
"I **want** to bury them underground."	he **wanted** to bury them underground.
"My father **gave** me a sheepskin coat."	his father **had given** him a sheepskin coat.
"I **haven't found** the right shopping center."	he **hadn't found** the right shopping center.
"I **have been making** an inventory."	he **had been making** an inventory.
Ginny:	She said (that) . . .
"I **can't** throw anything away."	she **couldn't** throw anything away.
"Maybe I'**ll** stop buying so much stuff."	maybe she **would** stop buying so much stuff.

When you report information that is still true, the verb tense often remains the same.
Someone explained to me that this **is** what you call "performance art."

Here are some things people said about their possessions. Complete the sentences to report what they said. Compare with a partner. Do you know any people like these?

1. "I'm not at all materialistic – I have very few possessions."
   A friend of mine said that he *wasn't materialistic* and that he *had very few possessions* .
2. "My closets are all full, but I can't stop buying new clothes."
   Someone at work told me that her closets ____________ , but she ____________ .
3. "I'm always throwing things away. Once I threw out an antique vase by mistake."
   My aunt said that she ____________ and that once she ____________ .
4. "We're in debt because we've spent too much money on stuff for our apartment."
   My brother told his wife that they ____________ because they ____________ .
5. "I have a huge collection of comic books that I just don't have room for."
   One of my teachers told me that he ____________ .
6. "We'll have to have a yard sale to get rid of all the junk we've been buying at yard sales."
   My neighbors said they ____________ .
7. "I never throw things away. I just leave things in the garage."
   Years ago, my cousin told me he ____________ .

3 Speaking and listening Who's materialistic?

About you **A Pair work Discuss the questions. How materialistic are you?**

1. Do you like to have all the latest gadgets?
2. How thrifty are you? Are you careful with money?
3. Are you very attached to your possessions?
4. Have you ever gotten upset because you lost or broke something valuable?
5. Do you often buy things you don't need?

B 3.21 **Listen to Howard answer the questions above. Take notes on one thing he says in answer to each question. Then compare with a partner. How much detail can you remember?**

"Howard said that he wasn't really interested in gadgets at all."

1 Building vocabulary

A 3.22 Listen and read the questionnaire from a money magazine. What kind of money manager are you?

What kind of money manager are you?

Go through our checklist to find out. Tally your answers and read your profile.

	Yes	No
1. Do you have a **monthly budget** and **stick to** it?	☐	☐
2. Do you **keep track of** how much you spend each week?	☐	☐
3. Do you give yourself an **allowance** for special "treats"?	☐	☐
4. Do you **pay** all your **bills** on time?	☐	☐
5. Do you **set aside money** each month in a **savings account**?	☐	☐
6. Do you have a bank account that **pays** good **interest**?	☐	☐
7. Do you **invest money in** reliable **stocks** and **bonds**?	☐	☐
8. Have you **put** enough **money away** for "a rainy day"?	☐	☐
9. Do you **pay in cash** or **by check** to avoid **charging** too much to a **credit card**?	☐	☐
10. When you borrow money from friends or family, do you **pay** it **back** right away?	☐	☐
11. If you **took out** a **loan**, would you **pay** it **off** as soon as you could?	☐	☐
12. If you **got into debt**, would you know how to **get out of debt**?	☐	☐

0-6 **Yes** answers: You're relaxed about managing your money. You're not worried about how much money you have, but you might need to do something to get things under control.

7-12 **Yes** answers: You're very systematic and careful with your money. Managing your money is important to you. You might need to make sure it doesn't make you feel stressed.

Word sort **B** **Pair work** What are your money habits? Complete the chart with sentences. Use ideas from the questionnaire, and add your own. Compare with a partner.

I . . .	I don't . . .
have a monthly budget.	*invest money in stocks.*

"I have a monthly budget, but I don't always stick to it."

Vocabulary notebook p. 94

2 Building language

A 3.23 **Listen. What did the market researcher ask John? Practice the conversation.**

John: I was stopped by one of those market researchers today. She was doing a survey on money.
Mother: Really? What kind of things was she asking?
John: She wanted to know whether I was a spender or a saver and how I usually paid for things.
Mother: Hmm. Did you tell her I pay for everything?
John: Uh, no. . . . Anyway, then she asked me how many times I'd used a credit card in the past month. I told her I didn't have one, and the next thing I knew, she asked if I wanted to apply for one!
Mother: But you're only 18!
John: Well, I filled out the application anyway. The only thing is, . . . she asked if a parent could sign it, so . . .

Figure it out **B** **How would John report these questions? Write sentences starting with** ***She asked me . . .***

1. Are you a regular saver?
2. Do you want a credit card?
3. How many times have you spent too much?
4. Can you sign this form?

3 Grammar Reported questions 3.24

Extra practice p. 148

Direct questions	**Reported questions**
The market researcher:	She asked (me) . . . / She wanted to know . . .
"**Are** you a spender or a saver?"	if / whether I **was** a spender or a saver.
"How **do** you usually **pay** for things?"	how I usually **paid** for things.
"How many times **have** you **used** a credit card?"	how many times **I'd used** a credit card.
"**Can** one of your parents **sign** the application?"	if / whether one of my parents **could sign** it.

A **Imagine the market researcher asked you these questions. Write reported questions.**

1. "What is your main source of income?"
   She asked me what my main source of income was.
2. "Are you relaxed about spending money?"
3. "Do you usually pay in cash, or do you often charge things to a credit card?"
4. "Can you stick to a monthly budget?"
5. "Have you taken anything back to a store recently?"
6. "How many times have you borrowed money from friends or family?"
7. "How much money can you spend on treats each month?"
8. "Do you have any loans? Are you paying them off as soon as you can?"

Common errors

Use statement word order in reported questions.

She asked how ***I usually paid*** *for things.*
(NOT *She asked how ~~did I usually pay~~ for things.*)

About you **B** **Pair work** **Take turns reporting the questions and giving your answers.**

"She asked me what my main source of income was, and I told her it was my parents!"

Sounds right p. 139

He was telling me . . .

1 Conversation strategy Reporting the content of a conversation

A Do you agree with the saying, "Money can't buy happiness"? Tell the class.

B 3.25 Listen. What does Lucy know about Jeff and Lee?

Lucy I ran into Max last week. He was telling me that Jeff and Lee aren't getting along that well. They've only been married six months. Apparently, they're having money problems.

Omar But I heard they're pretty wealthy. Or so someone was telling me.

Lucy Yeah, well, evidently the honeymoon and the diamond ring and everything were all paid for on credit cards. Max was telling me that Lee had no idea they were in debt.

Omar Really? How could she *not* know? There's got to be something wrong, you know, if she had no idea what was going on.

Lucy Yeah, that's what Max was saying. He went to see them, and he was saying how much stuff they have in their house. But as he said, "Money can't buy happiness."

Omar Obviously not.

C Notice how Lucy talks about her conversation with Max. She uses past continuous reporting verbs to focus on the content rather than the actual words she heard. Also, she generally doesn't "shift" tenses. Find examples.

"Max was telling me that Jeff and Lee aren't getting along that well."

D Imagine people you know said the things below. Rewrite the sentences to report what they said. Use past continuous reporting verbs.

1. A friend of yours: "I'm saving up to buy a car. I want a little two-seater sports car."
   A friend of mine was telling me she's saving up to buy a car. She was saying . . .
2. Your classmate: "My fiancée and I are going to have a small wedding. We decided big weddings are a waste of money. We'd rather have a nice honeymoon, so we've set aside some money for a trip to Sydney."
3. Your neighbors: "We want to put in a new kitchen, but we're going to have to take out a loan to pay for it. It's expensive."
4. Your co-worker: "I'm thinking of leaving my job and going back to school. I want to become a teacher. I think I'll be happier in that kind of a job than I am now."

About you **E Pair work** What have people told you recently? Tell a partner.

2 Strategy plus Quoting information

When you quote information you've heard, use these expressions to identify the source:
Max was telling me / was saying / told me . . .
(As) he said, ". . ." According to Max, . . .

Use these when you don't identify the source:
Apparently, . . . Evidently, . . .
I was told . . . I('ve) heard . . .
They say . . . I('ve) read . . .

Pair work **Discuss the questions. Use the expressions above in your answers to talk about what you've heard or read.**

1. Who's the richest person in the world?
2. What's a good way to invest money?
3. What's the best way to set money aside for college?
4. What's the quickest way to make a million dollars?
5. Which businesses have been successful in your city?
6. What's the most expensive thing you think you'll ever buy?
7. What's the best way to keep track of your spending?
8. Which jobs pay the best salaries? the worst?
9. Where's a good place to get a part-time job?

A ***Isn't it Carlos Slim Helú? I've heard he's worth billions.***
B ***Yeah. My friend was telling me there are a lot of billionaires in Mexico now.***

3 Speaking naturally Finished and unfinished ideas

	Finished idea:	**Unfinished idea:**
Sue was telling me about her job.	*It pays really* ***well.***	*It pays really* ***well*** *. . .*

A 3.26 **Listen and repeat the sentences above. Notice how the intonation falls to show the speaker has finished an idea and rises to show there's more to say.**

B 3.27 **Listen. Which of these sentences are finished ideas (F)? Which sound unfinished (U)? Write *F* or *U*.**

1. Dan was telling me about his new career ____
2. Evidently he's quit his job ____
3. He has no other source of income ____
4. He's trying to sell his art online ____
5. It all seems a little risky to me ____
6. I hope it pays off for him in the end ____

C 3.28 **Now listen to the full extract, and check your answers. Do you think Dan's situation is risky?**

About you **D** **Group work** **What are some good ways to make money? Which jobs pay well? Which don't? Tell your group about things you've heard and read.**

"My sister was telling me her boyfriend is a stockbroker. Apparently, he makes a fortune."

Do I really need that?

1 Reading

A Have you ever bought things that you don't use? What are they? Tell the class.

B Read the article. What was Leda's problem? What did she do about it?

Reading tip

Journalistic feature articles and blogs sometimes pretend to "speak" to the reader, e.g., *You know what?* Don't do this in academic writing.

http://www.leda...

ABOUT ME | FASHION & BEAUTY | **HOME & DESIGN** | FOOD & DRINK | TRAVEL | CONTACT ME | FAQS | PHOTO GALLERY | OLDER POSTS

AT HOME with **Leda**

8:33 p.m. September 26

This Stuff's Gotta Go!

Apparently, we only use 20 percent of the stuff we own on a regular basis. The rest just sits in our drawers and closets, cluttering up our lives.

I'm sure that's true in my case. As of last month, every corner of my apartment was crammed with cardboard boxes, full of junk that I "could never live without." Most of those boxes I hadn't opened in years. And you know what? I hadn't missed any of it. Actually, I didn't even *remember* what was in those boxes.

And it wasn't just the boxes. I had closets overflowing with clothes I didn't wear, books I was attached to but never read, old electronics that no longer worked – in short, my home was full of clutter, and I didn't have room for it all.

I knew I had to get things under control, so I called up my friend Willow. You know, that super-organized, less-is-more kind of friend that many of us have? Yeah, her. She said that I should go through all of my belongings and make an inventory. She then told me I needed to give away or sell anything I had more than one of . . . like the *three* coffee pots I had. (*Three* coffee pots? How did I even *get* three coffee pots?) Finally, Willow asked me how often I used my things. She explained that she keeps her home clutter-free by getting rid of anything that she hasn't worn or used in the last year. She added that I could keep things that had sentimental value, as long as they were *really* important and special.

So, in the past month, I've gotten rid of more than TWENTY boxes of junk and bags of clothes. Some of it I donated, recycled, or trashed, but most of it I sold. Decluttering has been an enormous task, but it has felt great to reclaim the space in my home again. And the best part? The cash I earned helped me pay off my credit card debt – something I had, no doubt, because I had bought too much stuff in the first place. ☺

C Read the article again. Are these sentences true or false? Check (✓) the boxes. Find the sentences in the article that support your answers.

	True	False
1. The writer says people use most of their things on a regular basis.	☐	☐
2. She used to think she needed most of the things in her boxes.	☐	☐
3. She had plenty of space in her closet for her clothes.	☐	☐
4. The writer's friend, Willow, told her to make a list of her belongings.	☐	☐
5. Willow told her to keep one thing out of each box.	☐	☐
6. Willow believes you should only keep things you use and need.	☐	☐
7. The writer found decluttering difficult but is happy that she has done it.	☐	☐
8. The writer solved another problem with the money she made from selling her stuff.	☐	☐

About you **D** **Find expressions in the article to replace the underlined expressions below. Then ask and answer the questions with a partner.**

1. Do you think you use only 20 percent of your things regularly?
2. Do you have closets that are full of things you don't need?
3. Which of your possessions are you especially fond of?
4. Could you get rid of anything that has a deep, emotional meaning for you?
5. Have you ever tried to get rid of things you don't want in your home? Was it a big job?

2 Listening and writing I couldn't live without . . .

A 3.29 **Listen to four people talk about things they couldn't live without. What do they talk about? Why couldn't they live without these things? Complete the chart.**

	He / She couldn't live without . . .	because . . .
1. Bruno		
2. Diana		
3. Midori		
4. Max		

About you **B** 3.30 **Listen again to the opinions. Do you agree? Write a response to each person.**

1. ______________________________
2. ______________________________
3. ______________________________
4. ______________________________

C **Class activity** **Ask your classmates, "What's one thing you couldn't live without? Why?" Take notes on three interesting ideas.**

D **Read the Help note and the article below. Underline the verbs used for reporting speech. Then write an article about your classmates. Use both direct speech and reported speech.**

Home | Edit | Document Elements | Tables | Table Layout | Charts | Smart Art

Things my classmates couldn't live without

One of my classmates, Mieko, said she couldn't live without her violin. "It's my most valuable possession," she explained. She got her first violin at the age of six. "I was so excited," she recalled. She took lessons in school and practiced every day. She is now an accomplished violinist. "I couldn't live without it," she concluded.

Help note

Reporting verbs for direct and reported speech

- Saying and explaining:
  "It's valuable," she ***said / told me / explained****.*
  She ***said / told me / explained*** *that it was valuable.*
- Remembering:
  "I lost it once," she ***remembered / recalled****.*
  She ***remembered / recalled*** *that she had lost it once.*
- Adding and finishing:
  "I love my violin," she ***added / concluded****.*
  She ***added / concluded*** *that she loved her violin.*

E **Read a classmate's article. Then tell the class about something one of your classmates couldn't live without. Which thing is the most interesting or unusual?**

Free talk p. 134

Vocabulary notebook Get rich!

Learning tip *Collocations*

When you learn a new word, notice its *collocations* – the words that are used with it. In this example, *open* and *close a bank account* are collocations.

bank account: You can open and close a bank account.

1 Cross out the words that are *not* collocations of the verbs below.

make	a credit card / a budget / a living
apply for	a job / a credit card / a bill
open	a savings account / a restaurant / a debt
pay off	a debt / a budget / a loan
invest in	loans / bonds / stocks

In conversation

Talk about money

The top 10 verbs that collocate with ***money*** are *spend*, *save*, *earn*, *make*, *have*, *invest*, *get*, *pay*, *borrow*, and *owe*.

2 Write collocations for these words and expressions. How many ideas can you think of?

Find verbs for these nouns

an allowance	cash
a bank account	a discount
a bill	money
a budget	

earn / make / spend money

Find adjectives for these nouns

allowance	expense
account	job
a budget	

3 **Word builder** Find the meanings of the words and expressions below. Use them in a sentence.

credit limit due date interest rate nest egg overdrawn account

On your own

Make a wish list of your financial goals. What would you like to accomplish in the next 5 years? 10 years? 20 years?

Can Do! Now I can . . .

✓ I can . . . ? I need to review how to . . .

- ☐ talk about possessions and materialism.
- ☐ discuss money management.
- ☐ report things that people said.
- ☐ report questions that people asked.
- ☐ report the content of conversations I've had.
- ☐ quote other people or sources of information.
- ☐ understand an interview about possessions.
- ☐ understand people talking about what they couldn't live without.
- ☐ read a blog about decluttering.
- ☐ write a survey article about my classmates' possessions.

1 What would you have done?

A Complete the story using the correct forms of the verbs and expressions in the box.

apply for a credit card	get out of debt	invest money in	pay good interest	set aside money
✓get an allowance	have a budget	keep track of	pay in cash	take out a loan

When Andrew was growing up, he was careful with his money. He *got an allowance* every week from his parents, and because he wanted to go to college, he ____________ every month. He opened a savings account that ____________ , so his savings grew. When he started college, he didn't have much money, but he ____________ and stuck to it. He ____________ the money he spent, and when he bought things, he always ____________ .

But then, Andrew won $1 million in a lottery, and everything changed. He didn't ____________ stocks and bonds. Instead, he went on a spending spree. He bought a house, a car, designer clothes, and a laptop, and he spent a lot on travel and entertainment. Soon he had nothing left, so he ____________ and started charging his everyday expenses. To pay his college tuition fees, he ____________ , which he is still paying off. Andrew graduated from college and has a good job now, but he still hasn't ____________ .

B Answer the questions using past modals *would have*, *should have*, *could have*, *must have*, *might have*, or *may have*. Discuss your answers with a partner.

1. What should Andrew have done with the money he won?
2. Is there anything he shouldn't have done?
3. What would you have done differently? What wouldn't you have done?
4. How do you think he must have felt after he'd spent all the money?
5. Why do you think Andrew went on a spending spree?

C Pair work Take turns retelling Andrew's story. Use the expressions *Apparently*, *Evidently*, and *I heard that*. Does it remind you of similar stories? Share them using *That reminds me* or *That's like*.

2 How many words can you remember?

Complete the charts. How many words can you think of to describe personal qualities or emotions? Compare with a partner. Then ask and answer questions using words from your charts.

Nouns	Adjectives
honesty	*happy*

"Is honesty important to you?" *"Are you generally a happy person?"*

3 So what were they saying?

A Complete these quotations with a problem and then add a solution, using the appropriate form of the verb given.

1. John: "I went rock climbing, and I got this really big _hole / tear_ in my backpack. It needs _to be sewn / sewing_ (sew). Are you good at sewing?"
2. Alice: "My kitchen faucet keeps ____________, and I can't turn it off. It needs ____________ (fix), but I can't afford to get a plumber ____________ (do) it right now. Can you take a look at it?"
3. Robert: "I have this big oil ____________ on my good jacket. I have to have it ____________ (clean) before my job interview next week. Which dry cleaner's has the fastest service?"
4. Maria: "My watch has been running ____________. I've never had the battery ____________ (change), so it probably needs ____________ (replace). How much will a new battery cost?"
5. Hilary: "I had a car accident, and one of my doors got a big ____________ in it. I've been looking for a place to get it ____________ (fix). Who fixed your car after your accident?"

B Report the general content of each person's problem, using *was saying (that)* or *was telling me (that)*. Then report exactly what the person said and asked about the solution, shifting the tenses back.

"John was saying that he got a hole in his backpack when he went rock climbing. He said that it needed to be sewn, and then he asked if I was good at sewing!"

4 Want some help?

A Complete the conversations with words like *Yuck*, *Ow*, *Ouch*, *Oops*, *Ooh*, *Ugh*, *Uh-oh*, and *Shoot*. Sometimes more than one answer is possible. Then practice with a partner.

1. A _Ow!_ I just got an electric shock. I should get that iron fixed.
   B ________ I bet that hurt. Are you OK?
2. A ________ My computer just crashed again. I can't understand it. It keeps happening.
   B ________ Maybe you have a virus. Do you want me to look at it?
3. A ________ I'm hungry. Do you want a snack?
   B Sure. Let's see. Do you want some scrambled eggs?
   A ________ I can't stand eggs.
   B ________ I just dropped them. Oh, well, never mind.
4. A ________ I forgot to hand in my homework today.
   B ________ Will your teacher be mad?
   A Probably. ________ look, it's all messed up. And oh ________. There's chewing gum stuck to it.

B Pair work Make each sentence shorter if possible, and practice again. Can you continue the conversations?

A Ow! Just got a shock. I should get that fixed.
B Ouch! Bet that hurt. You OK?
A Yeah. Think so. Guess I ought to . . .

UNIT 10

Fame

Can Do! In this unit, you learn how to . . .

Lesson A
- Talk about celebrities' rise to fame
- Use *if* clauses to say how things might have been different

Lesson B
- Talk about achieving and losing fame
- Use tag questions to give opinions or check information

Lesson C
- Use tag questions to soften advice and give encouragement
- Answer difficult questions with expressions like *It's hard to say*

Lesson D
- Read an article about child stars
- Write a profile of a successful person

1 Duke and Duchess of Cambridge

2 Usain Bolt
Olympic gold medalist

3 Ang Lee
Film director

4 J.K. Rowling
Author

5 Javier Bardem
Actor

Before you begin . . .
- What are some ways that people become famous?
- What do you think is the best thing about being famous?
- What is the worst thing about being famous?

Lesson A The rise to fame

http://www.watsoninfo...

A lucky break

Russell Watson's rise to fame was remarkable and unexpected. The English-born tenor had no formal music training, was an average student, and quit school at 16 to work in a factory. To make extra money, he sang in pubs in his spare time. Several years later, he sang in a radio talent contest and won, and his life took an amazing turn. He quit his job, got a manager, and started singing in clubs full-time. One night he ended a set of pop songs with an aria from an opera and got a standing ovation. He realized he was on to something. That's how he became a famous singer. By the age of 28, he had released his first album, *The Voice*, and had become an international star.

Comments

Dennis
I think it's a good thing he entered that contest. If he hadn't won, he might not have had the confidence to become a singer. And what would have happened if he had stayed in school? Maybe he would have done something entirely different.

Stephanie
Well, it's hard to know for certain, but I think he would have found a way to be a singer anyway. In fact, if he had continued his education, he could have had formal training and gotten an earlier start as a singer.

Anne
You might be right, Stephanie, but it was pretty brave of him to quit his job. If he hadn't quit and gotten a manager, he might not have had a singing career at all. What amazes me, though, is that he had enough nerve to sing something from an opera in a club! If he had only sung pop songs, he wouldn't have realized how much people loved his opera voice.

1 Getting started

A What kinds of talent contests can you enter? Would you enter one?

B Read the article "A lucky break" above. How did Russell Watson get his start as a professional singer?

C 4.01 Listen to the comments that people posted on the website about Russell Watson's career. Which comments do you agree with?

Figure it out **D** Can you complete the sentences below? Compare with a partner.

1. If Russell Watson had stayed in school, maybe he ____________ had a very different career.
2. If he ____________ won that talent contest, he might not have become a singer.
3. If he had only sung pop songs, he ____________ known people loved his opera voice.
4. What ____________ happened if he had only sung pop songs?

2 Grammar Talking hypothetically about the past 4.02

Extra practice p. 149

You can use sentences with *if* to talk hypothetically about the past.
Use the past perfect form in the *if* clause and a past modal in the main clause.

***If* + past perfect**	**Past modal *would have*, *could have*, *might have*, etc.**
If Watson **had stayed** in school,	maybe he **would have done** something entirely different.
If he **hadn't won** the talent contest,	he **might not have had** the confidence to become a singer.
If he **had continued** his education,	he **could have gotten** formal music training.

Hypothetical questions about the past
What **would have happened if** he **had stayed** in school?
What **would** he **have done if** he **hadn't won** the talent contest?
Would he **have become** a singer?

In conversation

People often say ***If I would have*** instead of ***If I had***, but this is not considered correct in writing.

Common errors

Use *if* + past perfect, not simple past.

*If he **hadn't quit** his job, he wouldn't have become a singer.*
(NOT *If he ~~didn't quit~~ his job . . .*)

A **Read the extract about a woman who became famous through the Internet. Then complete the sentences using the verbs given.**

Rebecca Black became an online sensation when her mother paid a record company to produce a music video of her daughter singing a song called "Friday." The video was uploaded onto a video-sharing website and watched by millions of people. Many music critics and viewers didn't like it, and some people called it "the worst song ever." Black appeared on several talk shows, and "Friday" soon became the most-watched video of the year. Black became a "viral star" and is now a successful artist.

1. If Rebecca's mother *hadn't paid* (not pay) the record company, they *wouldn't have produced* (not produce) the video, and they ____________ (not upload) it.
2. If the record company ____________ (not upload) the video, millions of people ____________ (not watch) it, and Rebecca ____________ (might not become) a viral star.
3. What ____________ (happen) if the song ____________ (got) good reviews? ____________ Black ____________ (become) famous if more people ____________ (like) the song? It's hard to tell, but it ____________ (might receive) less media attention.
4. If Black ____________ (not have) all the bad publicity, her music career ____________ (might not take) off. She ____________ (miss) out if she ____________ (listen) to all the critics.

About you **B** **Write about two things that have happened to you. Use the ideas below or your own. How would your life have been different if these things hadn't happened?**

a job you got   a person you met   something fun that happened to you   a trip you took

Getting my current job is one of the best things that has happened to me. If my friend hadn't told me about the job, I wouldn't have gotten it. If I had stayed in my old job, . . .

C **Pair work** **Take turns talking about each situation. Ask your partner questions for more information.**

Lesson B In the public eye

1 Building vocabulary and grammar

A 4.03 **Listen. How did Lana become famous? Practice the conversation.**

Jon Look. Lana's at the Swan Club! You haven't seen her show yet, have you?
Kylie No, but I'd love to go. . . . She's a blues singer, isn't she?
Jon Actually, she's an **up-and-coming** rock star. She's been **in the headlines** a lot recently.
Kylie Really? I guess I'm a little out of touch, aren't I?
Jon She was on that talent show, and since then, her **career**'s really **taken off**.
Kylie Oh, I know who she is! She won the show this year, didn't she?
Jon Yeah, she did. Last year she was a student, and now she's **making headlines** as a rock singer. It's amazing, isn't it?
Kylie Huh. She must have **had connections**.
Jon I don't think so. She **got discovered** in a karaoke club by one of the show's producers. She was just **in the right place at the right time**.
Kylie I wonder what happened to the guy who won last year – Java Thomas. He's kind of **dropped out of sight**, hasn't he?
Jon Well, he **got** a lot of **bad press** when he got caught shoplifting.
Kylie Shoplifting? That wasn't too smart, was it?
Jon No, it wasn't, and his **career** has really **gone downhill**.

Word sort **B** **Complete the chart using expressions in the conversation. Then tell a partner about someone famous. What do you know about him or her?**

Ways to become famous	When you're becoming famous	When things don't work out
You get *discovered* by someone. You're just in ____________ . You have ____________ .	Your career ____________ . You make ____________ . You're ____________ a lot. You're an ____________ star.	Your career ____________ . You get bad ____________ . You ____________ of sight.

Vocabulary notebook p. 106

Figure it out **C** **How would Jon and Kylie make these statements into questions?**

1. Lana's a singer, ____________ ?
2. She won a talent show, ____________ ?
3. Java Thomas wasn't too smart, ____________ ?
4. His career hasn't taken off, ____________ ?

2 Speaking naturally Intonation of tag questions

You're not sure and want to check something:	You're sure and think someone will agree:
You haven't seen her show yet, have you?	*It's amazing, isn't it?*

4.04 **Listen and repeat the questions above. Notice how the intonation rises or falls depending on the purpose of the question. Then practice Jon and Kylie's conversation again.**

3 Grammar Tag questions 4.05

Extra practice p. 149

Tag questions are statements followed by short questions in the same tense, called "tags."

Affirmative statement + negative tag
It's amazing, **isn't it?**
That was a dumb thing to do, **wasn't it?**
She won the talent show, **didn't she?**
He's dropped out of sight, **hasn't he?**

Answer *yes* to agree.
She won the talent show, **didn't she?**
Yes, she did.

Negative statement + affirmative tag
It's not easy to become famous, **is it?**
That wasn't too smart, **was it?**
She didn't have connections, **did she?**
His career hasn't taken off, **has it?**

Answer *no* to agree.
That wasn't too smart, **was it?**
No, it wasn't.

In conversation
Negative tags are much more frequent than affirmative tags.

A Complete the conversations with tag questions.

1. A You've heard of Chris Martin, ______________ ?
   B I think so. He sings with Coldplay, ______________ ?
   A Yeah. He's their lead singer.
   B Right. They're not American, ______________ ?
   A No, they're British. I love their music. They're a great band, ______________ ?
   B Oh, yeah. They've raised a lot of money for charity, too, ______________ ? I mean, they do a lot of charity concerts and stuff, ______________ ?
   A Yeah. I went to one. It was amazing.

2. A When was Marilyn Monroe famous? It was in the 1950s, ______________ ?
   B Yeah, but she made a movie in the 1960s, too, ______________ ?
   A I think you're right. She was mainly a movie star, ______________ ? I mean, she wasn't a singer, ______________ ?
   B Well, she sang in some of her movies, but she was basically an actress. You've seen her movies, ______________ ?
   A No, but I'd like to. It's amazing, ______________ ? She died years ago, but she's still famous.

B Pair work How would *you* say the tags above: with rising intonation (you're checking), or with falling intonation (you think your partner will agree)? Practice the conversations.

4 Talk about it Who's hot? Who's not?

Group work Discuss the questions. Who knows the most about people in the news?

- Where do you find out the latest celebrity news?
- Who's in the headlines these days? Why? Is anyone getting bad press?
- Who are the up-and-coming celebrities right now? Whose careers have taken off recently? Why?
- Can you think of any stars who have dropped out of sight? Why do you think their careers went downhill?

Sounds right p. 139

Good question!

1 Conversation strategy Giving encouraging advice

A What advice would you give a friend who is not learning much from a class? Make a list of ideas.

B 4.06 Listen. What is Nela's problem, and what is Steve's advice?

Steve So, how's your acting class going?

Nela It's hard to say. It's fun, but I'm not learning much.

Steve Well, you could look for another class, couldn't you?

Nela Maybe. The thing is, I like the teacher, but she hardly notices me. She never gives me any feedback.

Steve Hmm. How can you get her attention?

Nela Good question. I wish I knew. Actually, I'm thinking of dropping out.

Steve Well, before you do that, it would be good to talk with her, wouldn't it?

Nela I'm not sure I want to know what she thinks! I mean, most of the other students have been acting since they were kids. Do you think that if I'd gotten an earlier start, I'd be a better actor by now?

Steve That's a tough one. I don't know. But you've only been in the class a few weeks. You should at least give it a chance, shouldn't you?

Nela You're right. I guess I should.

C Notice how Steve uses tag questions to soften his advice and give Nela encouragement. Find examples in the conversation.

"You could look for another class, couldn't you?"

D Match the problems and advice. Then role-play the conversations, and take turns giving your own advice.

1. I'd really like to record my own podcast. But I'm not sure what topic to choose. _____
2. I really want to be a contestant on one of those TV game shows. But I'm not sure what kind of people they're looking for. _____
3. If I'd had formal training when I was young, I think I could have been a singer. _____
4. I'd like to act in a college play, but I get scared when I perform in front of people. _____

a. Well, it's never too late. You could still get voice lessons now, couldn't you?
b. It would help if you just practiced speaking out loud at home, wouldn't it? That might help with stage fright.
c. Well, you should pick something you know about, shouldn't you? Or something that interests you.
d. You could just look online, couldn't you? Though I bet they want confident people. Or people with a sense of humor.

2 Strategy plus *It's hard to say.*

You can use expressions like these when a question is difficult to answer.

It's hard to say.
(That's a) Good question.
That's a tough one.

About you **Pair work** **Ask and answer the questions. Use the expressions above if the question is difficult.**

1. Would you like to be famous? Why or why not?
2. How would being famous change your lifestyle?
3. Do you think being famous would change you as a person? How?
4. If you became famous, would you keep all of your old friends?
5. They say everyone gets 15 minutes of fame. What would you like to be famous for?
6. What would you have done if you hadn't continued your education?

A ***Would you like to be famous?***
B ***Well, good question. I mean, it could be exciting. But I think I'd get tired of all the attention.***

3 Listening and strategies Great advice

A 4.07 **Look at some advice for making a band successful. What else could you do? Then listen to Tom talk to George about his band. Check (✓) the things Tom needs to do.**

- ☐ practice more
- ☐ write more new songs
- ☐ play more "gigs"
- ☐ contact the local radio station
- ☐ record music and put it online
- ☐ get a manager
- ☐ choose a catchy name for the band

B 4.07 **Listen again. Answer the questions. Circle *a* or *b*.**

1. What kinds of songs does the band play?
   a. their own original songs b. other bands' songs
2. Where have they played?
   a. at local colleges b. at one or two big clubs
3. What does George think about getting the band's name known?
   a. He says it's hard. b. He thinks it's easy.
4. What does Tom think of his band's name?
   a. It's a cool name. b. He doesn't really like it.

About you **C** **Imagine you want to become famous. Choose an idea below or think of your own. What would you like to achieve? What problems would you face? Make a list.**

become an athlete | start a band | go on a TV show | create a popular blog

D **Pair work** **Discuss your ideas. Take turns giving advice.**

A ***Actually, I already write a blog, but I would like to get a wider audience. How do you do that?***
B ***Well, that's a tough one. It would help if you added some useful links to your blog, wouldn't it?***

Lesson D Rising stars

1 Reading

A **Can you think of any child stars? How do you think their lives are different from other children's lives?**

B **Read the magazine article. What is "Child Star Syndrome"? How have some actors coped with it?**

Reading tip

Writers often use words like *some*, *others*, and *many* to avoid repeating the same noun (e.g., child actors).

Three Child Stars Who Beat the Odds

"Child Star Syndrome"

So many former child actors reach their teens and end up in the headlines as they lose control of their lives. Some face pressure from parents and spend their early years working long hours, trying to achieve stardom. Others are unable to manage all the money, attention, and the glamorous lifestyle as they get older. Many simply find it difficult to grow up under the scrutiny of the media, and as they become adults, their careers often go downhill, or they eventually drop out of sight. However, not all child stars fail under the pressures of fame. Some have shown that it *is* possible to balance an acting career with a normal life.

Natalie Portman: In the Right Place at the Right Time

Actress Natalie Portman was 11 when she got discovered by an agent in a pizza shop. She became well known for her role in the *Star Wars* series beginning in 1999. The support of Portman's parents helped keep her life stable. They encouraged her to concentrate on her education even when she was traveling and filming. She even skipped the premiere of her first blockbuster movie to study for high school exams. In 2000, Portman took time off from acting to focus on her studies, and in 2003, she received a degree in psychology from Harvard University. After graduation, she starred in several movies, and in 2010, she won an Academy Award for her performance in the movie *Black Swan*. She admits that nothing is more important than her family life.

The Talented Young Stars of *Harry Potter*

English-born Daniel Radcliffe and Emma Watson were barely 11 years old when they began acting in the world-famous *Harry Potter* series in 2001. Fame and fortune certainly changed their lives, but with the support of their families (their parents were never impressed by fame) and the other actors on the set, they had healthy childhoods. Both Watson and Radcliffe earned excellent grades in school, and Watson was accepted into Brown University in Rhode Island and later Oxford University. As young adults, neither of them was interested in the glamorous lifestyle that their wealth would allow them to have. Their down-to-earth attitude hasn't stopped their ambitions, though. Both have secured leading roles in movies and the theater.

What's Their Secret?

If these actors hadn't had the support of parents and other adults, and if they hadn't had a high level of maturity, strength, and confidence, they might not have become the successful adult actors they are today. They've managed to cope extraordinarily well with the pressures of fame – a great achievement when you consider what could have gone wrong in their young lives.

C **Find words and expressions in the article to replace the underlined words in the questions. Then ask and answer the questions with a partner.**

1. What can happen to child actors who grow up in the public eye?
2. Is it possible to combine an acting career with an education?
3. What very successful movies has Natalie Portman starred in?
4. What did Portman decide to concentrate on in 2000?
5. How old were the *Harry Potter* stars when filming began – 10, or only just 11?
6. What types of parts have Daniel Radcliffe and Emma Watson managed to get?

D Which of these ideas does the article suggest? Check (✓) the boxes.

- ☐ All child actors have problems as they grow up.
- ☐ It is possible to be both a successful child and adult actor.
- ☐ Portman's career went downhill for a while.
- ☐ If Portman's parents hadn't made her study, she would have failed school.
- ☐ Radcliffe and Watson were both good students.
- ☐ As adults, all these former child actors are still successful.
- ☐ These actors became successful only due to the support of their parents.

2 Speaking and listening Success is . . .

A Pair work How do you define success? Discuss the ideas below and add your own.

being famous	having an important job	finding the right partner
enjoying life every day	doing fulfilling work	having lots of money

"I think you're successful if you become famous."

B 4.08 Listen to four people talk about success. What does success mean to them? Complete the sentences with ideas from above.

1. For Isabel, success is ______________.
2. For Claire, success is ______________.
3. For Carlo, success is ______________.
4. For Vivian, success is ______________.

C 4.08 Listen again. Do they think they have achieved success? Complete the chart.

	Are they successful?	Why do they think they are or aren't successful?
1. Isabel	Yes / No	______________
2. Claire	Yes / No	______________
3. Carlo	Yes / No	______________
4. Vivian	Yes / No	______________

3 Writing A success story

A Think of someone you know who has achieved success in some way. Make a list of reasons why he or she became successful. Then write a paragraph about him or her.

Home | Edit | Document Elements | Tables | Table Layout | Charts | Smart Art

My successful friend

My friend Alexis is already a successful doctor at the age of 30, even though she had a difficult childhood in many ways. Her parents divorced when she was three, and she spent her early years moving from town to town and school to school. . . .

Help note

Topic and supporting sentences

Topic sentences state an idea or a theme.

Supporting sentences add more information or give examples.

B Read your classmates' paragraphs. Are any of the stories inspiring?

Free talk p. 133

Learning tip *Learning idioms*

Idioms are expressions in which the meaning isn't obvious from the individual words. When you learn a new idiom, it helps to write an example sentence that explains or clarifies its meaning.

In conversation

Fame and fortune

The words most likely to be used with ***fame*** are:

1. fame ***and fortune***
2. ***gained*** fame
3. ***hall of*** fame
4. ***claim to*** fame
5. ***achieved*** fame

1 Match these sentences containing idioms with the explanations on the right.

1. He's been in the headlines a lot lately. c
2. He's getting a lot of bad press. ____
3. He's an up-and-coming actor. ____
4. His career has really taken off. ____
5. He got discovered very young. ____
6. He had connections in the industry. ____
7. He's really dropped out of sight. ____
8. His acting career is going downhill. ____

a. His career is going really well.
b. People think he's going to be a great actor.
c. He's been in the news.
d. You don't hear about him anymore.
e. He knew people who helped his career.
f. He's getting fewer and fewer acting roles.
g. He started his career at a young age.
h. The news media are criticizing him.

2 Word builder Now write explanation sentences for these idioms. Find out the meaning of any expressions you don't know.

1. A lot of young people really look up to pop stars. ____________
2. My friend is a great singer. She's going to go a long way. ____________
3. Some rock bands are still going strong after 20 or 30 years. ____________
4. That young actor is going to make a name for himself. ____________
5. She knew the right people, so she got the part. ____________
6. He came to the city to try to get into show business. ____________

On your own

Make a list of 10 famous people you like. Can you use a different idiomatic expression about each person?

Can Do! Now I can . . .

✓ I can . . .   ? I need to review how to . . .

- ☐ talk hypothetically about the past.
- ☐ talk about celebrities and being famous.
- ☐ use tag questions to give opinions and check information.
- ☐ use tag questions to soften advice.
- ☐ answer difficult questions with expressions like *It's hard to say.*
- ☐ understand someone giving advice.
- ☐ understand people talking about success.
- ☐ read an article about child stars.
- ☐ write a profile of a successful person.

UNIT 11

Trends

Can Do! In this unit, you learn how to . . .

Lesson A
- Talk about social changes using the passive of the present continuous and present perfect

Lesson B
- Discuss the environment
- Use expressions like *although*, *because of*, *in order to*, and *instead*

Lesson C
- Use expressions like *As I said* to refer back in a conversation
- Use vague expressions like *and so forth*

Lesson D
- Read an article about success via the Internet
- Write a post for a website about technological trends

1

2

4

3

Before you begin . . .

Do any of these issues affect your city or country? Is the situation changing? What is the trend?

- traffic congestion
- work / life balance
- pollution
- an aging population
- urban development
- high unemployment

Lesson A Trends in society

What social changes have you noticed recently?

1 "A lot of people are obsessed with losing weight and eating healthy foods. So the fast-food chains have been forced to change their menus. Now you can get salads and healthy stuff there as well as burgers and fries. And that's a good thing because obesity has become a big problem."
– Jake,
New York City

2 "Well, people are talking about losing their jobs. In many places, unemployment is going up, and a lot of people have been laid off. And that's partly because their jobs are being outsourced to workers in other countries."
– Letitia,
Detroit

3 "I think, like everywhere else, the main thing is the spread of technology. I mean, almost everyone I know has a cell phone now . . . and wireless Internet access is being made available in more and more places."
– Daniela,
Monterrey

4 "We have a lot of problems with traffic congestion. Fortunately, a lot of new highways have been built, and there's a new monorail, but the problem hasn't been completely solved. So, commuting can still be a real problem."
– Somchai,
Bangkok

5 "Well, young people are still being encouraged to go to college, which is good. It can be tough, though, because tuition fees have just been increased, and we're not being given enough financial support."
– Oliver,
Manchester, UK

6 "Well, with the economic boom in recent years, one thing here is the shortage of skilled labor. There's a big demand for that now, so skilled workers are being recruited overseas, and then they're being brought in to fill the jobs."
– Ivan,
Moscow

1 Getting started

A Have any of these issues been in the news recently? Why? Tell the class.

____ college tuition fees	____ obesity	____ shortage of skilled workers
____ new technology	____ outsourcing jobs	____ traffic congestion

B 4.09 Listen. Which of the issues above are the people talking about? Number the issues 1 to 6.

Figure it out **C** How do the people express the ideas below? Rewrite the sentences.

1. They are encouraging young people to go to college.
2. They are not giving us enough financial support.
3. People have forced fast-food chains to change their menus.
4. They haven't completely solved the problem.

2 Grammar The passive 4.10

Extra practice p. 150

The passive of present continuous and present perfect

Use the active form of a verb to focus on the "doer" or cause of the action.	**Use the passive form to focus on the "receiver" of the action.**
Companies **are recruiting** workers overseas. They **are making** Internet access available.	Workers **are being recruited** overseas. Internet access **is being made** available.
Companies **have laid off** a lot of people. They **haven't solved** the traffic problem.	A lot of people **have been laid off**. The traffic problem **hasn't been solved**.

A **Rewrite the comments, using the passive forms of the underlined verbs. Then compare with a partner.**

That problem hasn't been solved yet. . . .

1. Teen car accidents are still a big concern for parents. They haven't solved that problem yet. However, they are advertising tracking devices. They've developed these devices to track speed. Some even turn the radio down. Apparently, they have saved a lot of lives.
2. They're providing healthier lunches in high schools now. They haven't taken junk food off menus completely. But they're not using processed food – well, not as much. Also, they're serving more organic foods.
3. They're developing the city center. They've knocked down a lot of older buildings, and they've built a lot of new hotels and offices. They're not solving the housing shortage, though. They're building too few homes.

About you **B** **Group work** **Discuss the different trends in this lesson. Which are good? Which are not? Which are happening where you live? What other trends are there?**

"Some roads in the city center are being closed to traffic. It's great. There are more outdoor cafés . . . "

3 Speaking naturally Reducing auxiliary verbs

*The education system **is** being reformed.*	*(system**'s** being)*
*The education system **has** been reformed.*	*(system**'s** been)*
*A lot of new schools **are** being built.*	*(schools**'re** being)*
*A lot of new schools **have** been built.*	*(schools**'ve** been)*

A 4.11 **Listen and repeat the sentences above. Notice the reduction of the auxiliary verbs.**

About you **B** 4.12 **Listen and complete the sentences. Are they true in your country? Are they good ideas? Discuss your views with a partner.**

1. More women ______________ encouraged to train as science and engineering teachers.
2. Bilingual programs ______________ offered to elementary school students.
3. Students ______________ required to do community service.
4. Education ______________ given more funding.
5. Technology ______________ introduced into more classrooms.
6. Courses ______________ made available for more people in the community.

Lesson B Environmental matters

1 Building vocabulary and grammar

A Complete the article with words and expressions from the box. What do you learn?

air pollution	drought	environmentally friendly	a landfill	toxic chemicals
biodegradable	energy-saving	global warming	✓natural resources	water consumption

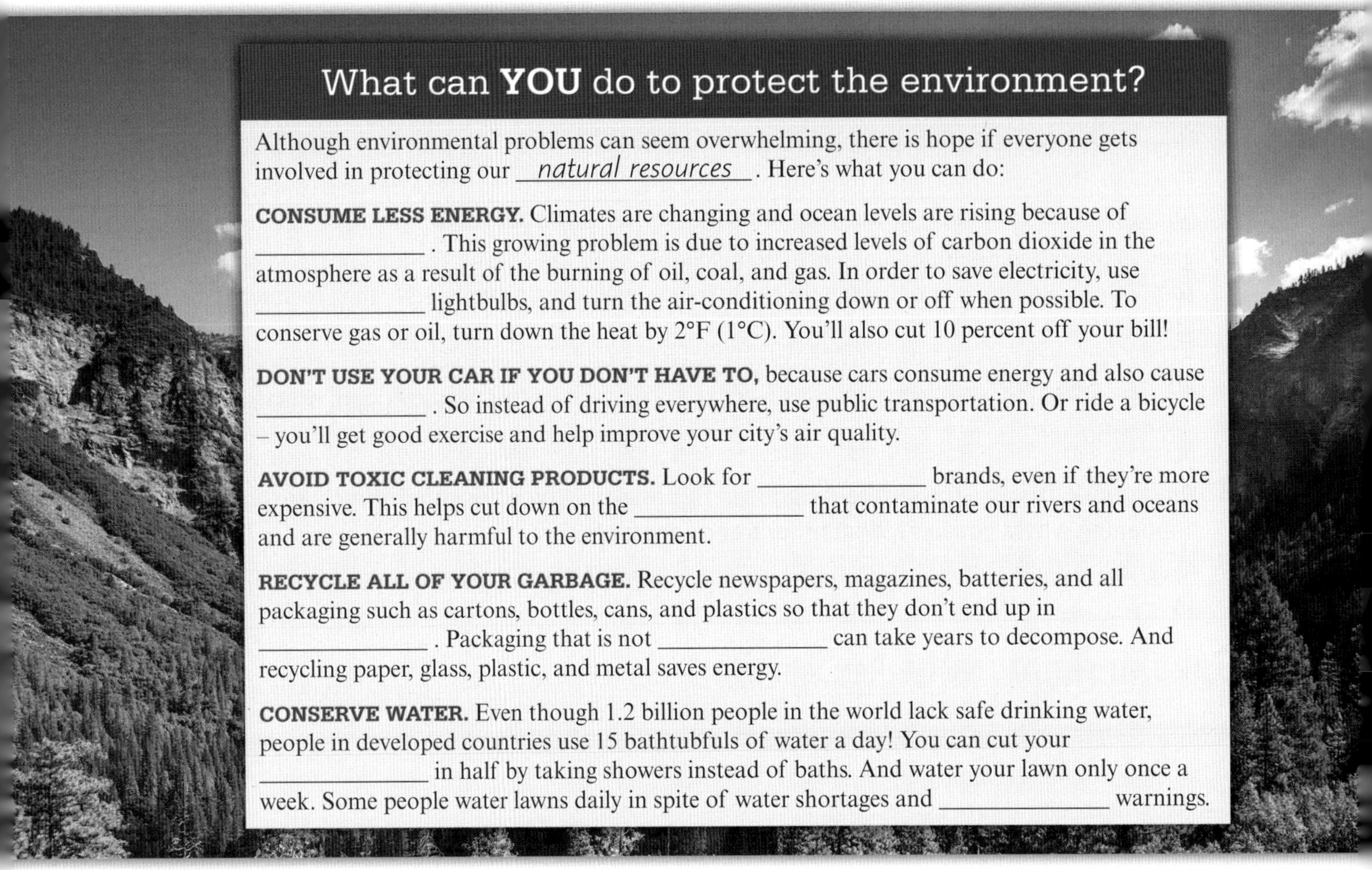

What can **YOU** do to protect the environment?

Although environmental problems can seem overwhelming, there is hope if everyone gets involved in protecting our *natural resources*. Here's what you can do:

CONSUME LESS ENERGY. Climates are changing and ocean levels are rising because of ______________. This growing problem is due to increased levels of carbon dioxide in the atmosphere as a result of the burning of oil, coal, and gas. In order to save electricity, use ______________ lightbulbs, and turn the air-conditioning down or off when possible. To conserve gas or oil, turn down the heat by 2°F (1°C). You'll also cut 10 percent off your bill!

DON'T USE YOUR CAR IF YOU DON'T HAVE TO, because cars consume energy and also cause ______________. So instead of driving everywhere, use public transportation. Or ride a bicycle – you'll get good exercise and help improve your city's air quality.

AVOID TOXIC CLEANING PRODUCTS. Look for ______________ brands, even if they're more expensive. This helps cut down on the ______________ that contaminate our rivers and oceans and are generally harmful to the environment.

RECYCLE ALL OF YOUR GARBAGE. Recycle newspapers, magazines, batteries, and all packaging such as cartons, bottles, cans, and plastics so that they don't end up in ______________. Packaging that is not ______________ can take years to decompose. And recycling paper, glass, plastic, and metal saves energy.

CONSERVE WATER. Even though 1.2 billion people in the world lack safe drinking water, people in developed countries use 15 bathtubfuls of water a day! You can cut your ______________ in half by taking showers instead of baths. And water your lawn only once a week. Some people water lawns daily in spite of water shortages and ______________ warnings.

Word sort **B** Which problems are you concerned about (or not)? What do you do, or not do? Make a chart like this with ideas from the article, and add your own. Compare with a partner.

I'm concerned about . . .	I'm not concerned about . . .
global warming. I don't use my car for short trips.	*conserving water. I take baths. I don't take showers.*

Vocabulary notebook p. 116

Figure it out **C** Can you choose the correct expression to complete each sentence? Compare with a partner. Are the sentences true for you?

1. I buy rechargeable batteries **in spite of / even though** the extra cost.
2. **Because / Because of** cars cause air pollution, I always take public transportation.
3. I turn down the air conditioning **in order to / so that** use less electricity.
4. I recycle cans **instead of / so** throwing them in the trash.

2 Grammar Linking ideas 4.13

Extra practice p. 150

Contrast	**Although / Even though** environmental problems are overwhelming, there is hope. Some people water their lawns daily **in spite of / despite** drought warnings.
Reason	Climates are changing **because of / as a result of / due to** global warming. Carbon dioxide levels are increasing **because** we are burning oil, coal, and gas.
Purpose	Turn down the air-conditioning **(in order) to** save electricity. Recycle garbage **so (that)** it doesn't end up in a landfill.
Alternative	Use public transportation **instead of** driving your car. Take showers **instead of** baths.

Notice:
***in order to / to* + verb**
***although / even though / because / so that / so* + clause**
***in spite of / despite / because of / as a result of / due to / instead of* + noun (or verb + *-ing*)**

A Link the ideas in these sentences using expressions from the grammar chart. How many ways can you complete each sentence? Compare with a partner.

Common errors

Don't write *even though* or *in spite of* as one word.

***Even though** fuel is expensive, I drive my car a lot.*
(NOT ~~*Eventhough*~~ *fuel is expensive, I drive my car a lot.*)

1. *Even though / Although* there are a lot of environmental problems, the situation isn't hopeless.
2. It's better to use everyday items to clean your home ____________ buying expensive cleaning products. For example, you can use vinegar to clean your mirrors ____________ toxic chemicals.
3. ____________ cut down on the paper you use, get all your bills delivered online.
4. A lot of vegetables from local areas are being sold in stores ____________ consumer pressure. This is good ____________ it supports local farmers and cuts down on transportation.
5. A lot of areas are being affected by air pollution ____________ efforts to improve air quality. Ride a bicycle or walk ____________ using the car. Or, if you buy a new car, get a hybrid vehicle ____________ you can save on gas.
6. If you buy bottled water, make sure the bottle is biodegradable ____________ you can prevent buildup in landfills.
7. There is more solar and wind power now ____________ advances in technology. However, ____________ recent advances, they're not being used as widely as they could be by consumers.
8. ____________ we need to preserve our natural resources, we also need to use oil and gas for energy.

About you **B Pair work Discuss the ideas above. Which ones do you agree with?**

3 Talk about it Saving the planet

Group work Discuss the environmental problems below. What other problems are there? Which are the most serious? What is being done to solve the problems? What else could be done?

- air and water pollution
- depletion of oil reserves
- garbage in landfills
- global warming
- nuclear waste disposal
- endangered species

A ***Even though air pollution is getting worse, not much is being done about it.***
B ***Well, "no-drive" days are being introduced in order to cut down on traffic on the worst days.***

Sounds right p. 139

As I was saying, . . .

1 Conversation strategy Referring back in the conversation

A Read the comment below. What other workplace trends are making companies family-friendly?

Adam *"I think there's a trend toward companies becoming family-friendly. For example, a lot of men are being offered paid leave when they become fathers."*

B 4.14 Listen. What other changes in the workplace do Adam, Celia, and Greg talk about?

Adam As I was saying, companies are definitely more family-friendly these days. And like I said, there's more paternity leave, flexible hours, child-care centers, and so on.

Celia Yeah. There are definitely more benefits and incentives for working parents. I think companies need to attract and keep good employees.

Greg Right. And going back to what you were saying about benefits, a lot more people are being encouraged to telecommute instead of working at the office.

Celia I think companies do it in order to save on costs. And with things like email, and web conferencing, and so forth, it's no problem.

Greg I'm sure they get increased productivity, too. Fewer interruptions, fewer meetings, etc.

Adam You mentioned earlier, Celia, about saving on costs. There seems to be a trend, too, toward offering internships to young people.

Celia Right. I mean, it's a great way to get experience and contacts, and so forth . . .

Greg Yeah, but basically it's just unpaid work.

C Notice how Adam, Celia, and Greg use expressions like these to refer back to things said earlier. Find examples.

You / I mentioned . . . earlier.

As / Like	*I said / I was saying . . .*
Going back to what	*you said / you were saying . . .*

D 4.15 Listen to more of the conversation. Write the expressions you hear. Then discuss the ideas with a partner. Do you agree with any of them?

Greg I mean, ____________, Celia, companies want to save on costs.

Celia But ____________, it's good experience. And internships can lead to full-time jobs.

Adam True. And companies can see if someone is a good fit before they hire them. ____________, Celia, they need good employees. It's ____________, people want good benefits.

Celia Right. And ____________, Greg, telecommuting is a kind of benefit.

2 Strategy plus *and so forth*

In more formal settings, use vague expressions like *and so forth*, *and so on*, and *etc.*, instead of informal expressions like *and things like that*.

etc. = et cetera

In conversation

Informal vague expressions like ***and things like that*** are more common than formal ones.

and things like that
and so forth
and so on
etc.

About you **Complete the sentences with the words in the box, and add a vague expression. Then discuss with a partner. Do you agree?**

equal pay	health insurance	improve their résumés	less time off	restaurants

1. Due to the state of the economy, people are being forced to work harder, with longer hours, ______________________ .
2. Companies should offer more benefits, like more vacation days, better ______________________ .
3. Men and women should be treated equally, with equal chances of promotion and ______________________ .
4. Young people do internships because of the opportunity they get to gain experience, ______________________ .
5. In order to survive, people are being forced to work into their 70s and 80s, in stores and ______________________ .

"People are being forced to work harder. Most people I know work late and work on the weekends, and so on."

3 Listening and strategies Trends in the workplace

A Look at the sentences below. Can you guess what else the people might say?

- ☐ As I was saying, working from home has some disadvantages, for example . . .
- ☐ Going back to what you were saying about desk sharing, it's good because . . .
- ☐ Going back to what you said about working flexible hours, it makes sense because . . .
- ☐ I mentioned earlier that calls and email are being monitored more. It's necessary . . .
- ☐ As I said, paternity leave isn't being offered in some companies, but . . .

B 4.16 Listen to extracts from four conversations. Which of the topics above are the people discussing? Number the sentences 1 to 4. There is one extra sentence.

C 4.16 Listen again. Write one advantage and one disadvantage of each trend.

About you **D Pair work Discuss each trend. What other advantages are there? What are other disadvantages? Which benefit would you most like to have?**

Free talk p. 135

Lesson D Technological change

1 Reading

A **How do people use the Internet to promote themselves? List as many ways as possible.**

"They post videos of their singing or acting."
"They create websites on a specific topic. They write interesting blogs."

Reading tip

As you read, ask yourself questions like, "Is this true?" "So, what does this mean?" "What examples can I think of?"

B **Read the article. What are the three people mentioned in the article famous for?**

http://www.internetsuccesses...

The Internet — The new pathway to success?

Years ago, the path to success in the world of entertainment seemed long and arduous. Aspiring artists often waited years before being noticed by the public. There were endless stories of actors waiting tables in Hollywood hoping to get discovered; of writers sending off hundreds of manuscripts to publishers only to accumulate a pile of rejection letters; of singers working for next to nothing in small clubs as they waited to get signed by a record company. Nowadays, however, instead of depending on big media companies to decide their future, more and more artists are following the trend of displaying their talents online – often with spectacular results.

Pop star Justin Bieber is perhaps the best-known Internet success story. This self-taught musician was a fifteen-year-old Canadian high school student whose only claim to fame was a second-place prize in a local talent show. When his mother began posting videos of Justin singing on the Internet, he became an "overnight sensation." Within months he was signing a contract with a major record label, and his first full-length album, *My World 2.0*, hit the charts around the world.

A growing number of novelists are gaining recognition on the Internet, too. That's where Darcie Chan self-published her first novel as an e-book even though it was rejected by ten publishers and more than a hundred literary agents. The novel, *The Mill River Recluse*, sold 400,000 copies in its first year. As a result of that success, Chan is now being courted by major publishers and even by movie studios.

A different sort of fame has been achieved by Michelle Phan, who got her start with online video tutorials on beauty and cosmetics. Within a few years, she had over 200 videos to her credit, and more than one *billion* Internet views. She has now been hired by a major cosmetics company to promote their products online.

Clearly, because of the Internet, talented people are increasingly less dependent on the power of the publishing, music, and movie industries. Of course, most stories of Internet success are much more modest. When a video of a cat playing the piano or a child singing opera goes viral, the fame doesn't last very long. As the artist Andy Warhol famously predicted in 1968: "In the future, everyone will be world-famous for 15 minutes." It's a prediction that certainly appears to be coming true. Who knows who or what trend will emerge in the next 15 minutes? Your guess is as a good as mine.

C **Rewrite the questions below, replacing the underlined words with similar expressions from the article. Then read the article again, and ask and answer the questions with a partner.**

1. When Justin Bieber was in high school, what was his <u>reason for being well known</u>?
2. Who helped Justin Bieber become <u>an instant success</u> on the Internet? How did it happen?
3. How did the Internet help Darcie Chan <u>become respected</u> as an author? What were the results?
4. How many video tutorials does Michelle Phan have <u>that she has made herself</u>? What evidence is there of her success?
5. What are some examples of Internet videos that <u>become extremely popular very quickly</u>?

D Pair work **Discuss the questions with a partner.**

1. What are some things aspiring artists used to do in order to get noticed? Name three things.
2. Do you know of other people who followed the same route to success as Justin Bieber, Darcie Chan, or Michelle Phan?
3. In what way is Andy Warhol's famous prediction coming true? Can you think of examples?
4. How will things change for publishers, record labels, and movie studios in the future?

2 Listening and writing Trends in technology

A 4.17 Listen to four people talk about recent trends. What trends are they talking about? Write *a* to *d*. Then decide if the person feels positive (P) or negative (N) about the trend. Circle *P* or *N*.

1. Adam ______ (P / N)
2. Emily ______ (P / N)
3. Tyler ______ (P / N)
4. Madison ______ (P / N)

a. home media systems
b. typing technology
c. phone use in social situations
d. online shopping

B 4.17 Listen again. Why does each person like or dislike the new trend? Write at least one reason.

1. Adam: ____________________
2. Emily: ____________________
3. Tyler: ____________________
4. Madison: ____________________

About you **C Pair work** **Think of a trend in technology that has affected you. How has it changed your life? Do you feel positive or negative about it? Write down some notes. Then discuss it with your partner.**

D Read the comment on a technology website and the Help note. Underline the expressions the writer uses to describe a trend. Then use your notes from Exercise C to write a similar post.

David128

posted 3 hours ago

The trend away from laptops

Recently I've noticed that my friends and I are spending less time on our laptops and more and more time on our smartphones. Phones used to be used mainly for texting and for taking and sending photos, while laptops were used for everything else, like answering email, watching videos, getting directions, or searching the Internet. As people increasingly use their smartphones for these functions, the use of laptops is declining. For me, at least, this is a good change. I used to carry a heavy laptop from café to café in order to access the Internet. Now I can go online without paying for an expensive cup of coffee!

Help note

Describing trends

*We're spending **more and more** time on our smartphones.*

*We're spending **less** time / **fewer** hours on our laptops.*

*People **increasingly** use their phones for a variety of functions.*

*The use of laptops is **decreasing** / **declining**.*

*The number of smartphones is **increasing** / **growing**.*

About you **E Group work** **Read your group's posts. Have you all noticed the same trends? Discuss.**

Learning tip *Writing definitions in your own words*

When you learn a new word or expression, you can write a definition or explanation in your own words to help you remember its meaning.

In conversation

It's in the air!

The type of pollution people talk about most is ***air pollution***.

1 **Match the expressions with their definitions or explanations.**

1. The **atmosphere** refers to _e_
2. **Carbon dioxide** is a gas in the atmosphere ____
3. If you **consume** something, ____
4. **Air quality** refers to ____
5. When there is a **water shortage**, ____
6. If something is **toxic** to the environment, ____
7. When you **recycle** something, ____
8. If something **decomposes**, ____

a. you use it up, and it can't be used again.
b. there isn't enough water for people.
c. you use it again instead of throwing it away.
d. it contaminates or pollutes the environment.
e. the air around the Earth.
f. that is produced when things burn or decay.
g. it decays, or breaks down into simple elements.
h. how much pollution is in the air.

2 **Write sentences that define or explain these words.**

air pollution	drought	global warming	toxic chemicals
biodegradable	environmentally friendly	a landfill	water consumption

3 **Word builder** **Find out the meaning of these words and expressions. Then write a sentence to define or explain each one.**

deforestation	fossil fuels	hybrid cars	pesticides
extinction	the greenhouse effect	the ozone layer	renewable energy

On your own

Post notes around your home in English reminding you to turn off the lights, recycle bottles, and so on.

Can Do! Now I can . . .

☑ I can . . . ? I need to review how to . . .

- ☐ talk about social changes.
- ☐ talk about environmental problems.
- ☐ link ideas with expressions like *although*, *because of*, *in order to*, and *instead.*
- ☐ refer back to points made earlier in the conversation.
- ☐ use formal vague expressions.
- ☐ understand a discussion about workplace trends.
- ☐ understand conversations about technology trends.
- ☐ read an article about success via the Internet.
- ☐ write a comment for a website about technological tre

UNIT 12

Careers

Can Do! In this unit, you learn how to . . .

Lesson A
- Discuss career planning using *What* clauses and long noun phrases

Lesson B
- Discuss job prospects
- Talk about your career plans using the future continuous and future perfect

Lesson C
- Introduce what you say with expressions like *What I read was*
- Say *I don't know if* . . . to introduce ideas

Lesson D
- Read an article on how to answer tough interview questions
- Write a cover letter for a job application

Before you begin . . .

Which of these areas of work are hard to get into? Which are easier? Which are the highest paid? Which are the most popular with your friends?

- the media
- travel and tourism
- medicine
- law
- finance
- entertainment
- social work
- teaching
- trades (carpentry, plumbing)

What's the best way to go about choosing a career?

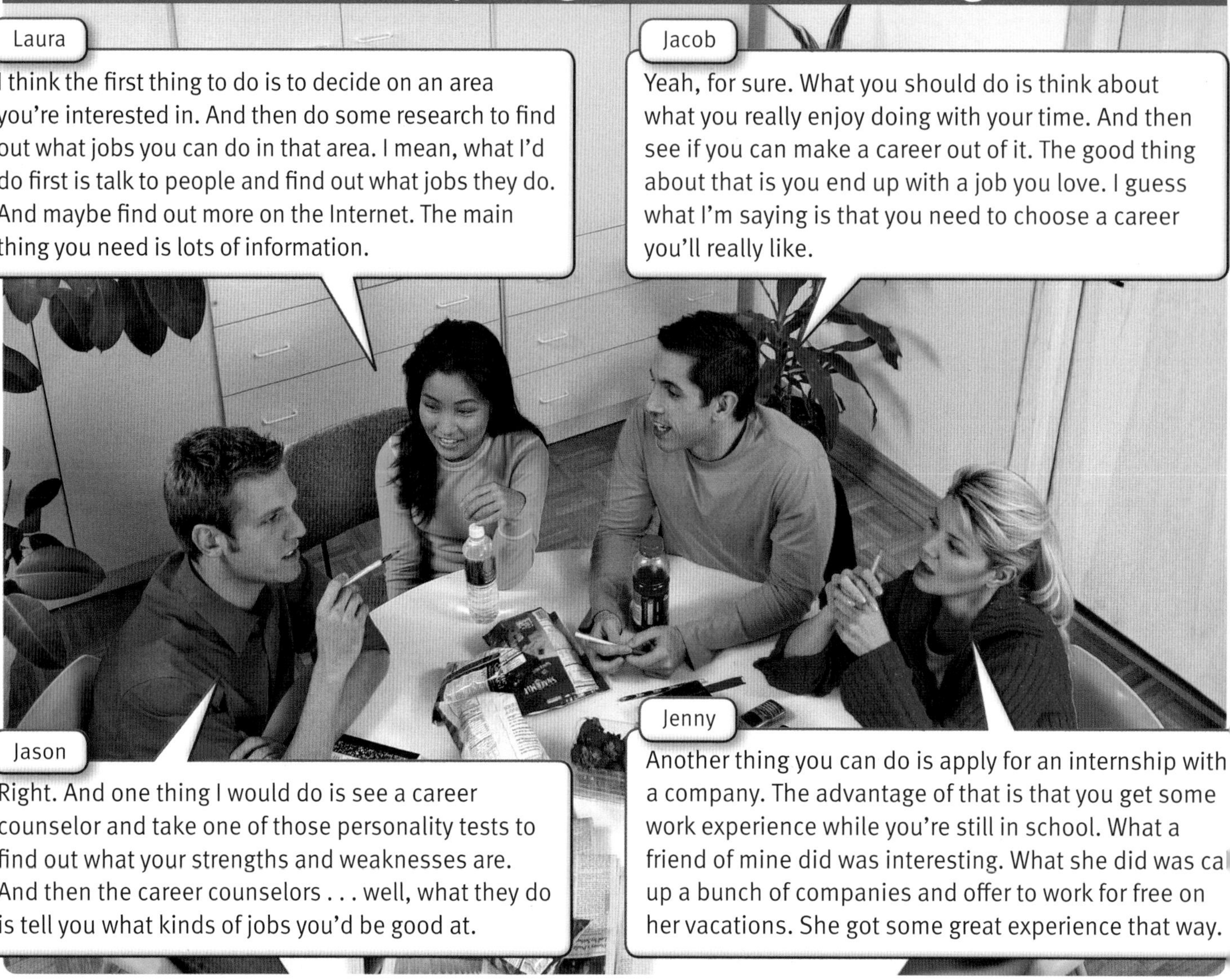

Laura
I think the first thing to do is to decide on an area you're interested in. And then do some research to find out what jobs you can do in that area. I mean, what I'd do first is talk to people and find out what jobs they do. And maybe find out more on the Internet. The main thing you need is lots of information.

Jacob
Yeah, for sure. What you should do is think about what you really enjoy doing with your time. And then see if you can make a career out of it. The good thing about that is you end up with a job you love. I guess what I'm saying is that you need to choose a career you'll really like.

Jason
Right. And one thing I would do is see a career counselor and take one of those personality tests to find out what your strengths and weaknesses are. And then the career counselors . . . well, what they do is tell you what kinds of jobs you'd be good at.

Jenny
Another thing you can do is apply for an internship with a company. The advantage of that is that you get some work experience while you're still in school. What a friend of mine did was interesting. What she did was ca up a bunch of companies and offer to work for free on her vacations. She got some great experience that way.

1 Getting started

A **Which of these do you think are the best three ways to choose a career? Tell the class.**

☐ do an internship
☐ talk to a career counselor
☐ do research online
☐ go to a job fair
☐ take a personality test
☐ ask a friend for advice

B 🔊 **4.18 Listen to four students talk about ways to choose a career. Which of the ideas above do they mention? Check (✓) the ideas. What other ideas do they suggest?**

Figure it out **C** **How do the people above say these things? Underline what they say in the discussion.**

1. Jenny A friend of mine did something interesting. She called up a bunch of companies.
2. Jacob I guess I'm saying that you need to choose a career you'll really like.
3. Laura First you need to decide on an area you're interested in.
4. Jason I would see a career counselor.

2 Grammar *What* clauses; long noun phrase subjects 4.19

Extra practice p. 151

***What* clauses and long noun phrases introduce important information. They are often the subject of the verb *be*, which can be followed by a word or a phrase (noun, adjective, or verb) or by a clause.**

***What* clauses**	**Long noun phrases**
What you need is lots of information.	**The main thing you need** is information.
What my friend did was interesting.	**Something my friend did** was interesting.
What I would do is talk to people.	**The best thing to do** is (to) talk to people.
What I'm saying is (that) you need to choose a career you'll really like.	**The good thing about that** is (that) you end up with a job you love.

A Choose the best expression on the right to complete each sentence.
Once you've chosen a career, how do you go about getting your dream job?

1. Well, ___*the best thing to do*___ is to make contacts and network with people. ______________ is ask all my friends and family if they know anyone who could help me. ______________ is it could help you get an interview.
   - the good thing about that
   - ✓the best thing to do
   - what I would do
2. ______________ is get some work experience. ______________ is it helps you find out if you'd really like a job in that area. ______________ is try it out first.
   - what I'm saying
   - the advantage of that
   - what I would do first
3. ______________ was get an internship. She said ______________ is a good reference letter. Then ______________ was interesting. She just walked into several different companies and introduced herself.
   - the main thing you need
   - something my friend did
   - what she did
4. ______________ is a good résumé. ______________ was good. She got hers done professionally. ______________ is you make a really good first impression.
   - the best thing about that
   - what my classmate did
   - what you need

About you **B Pair work** How would you go about getting your dream job? Discuss ideas.

A *What I'd do first is update my social networking site and say I'm looking for a job.*

B *That's a good idea. The best thing to do is tell all your contacts.*

3 Speaking naturally Stressing *I* and *you*

Anne *What would you do if you found your dream job and then hated it?*
Matt *I don't know. What would **you** do if **you** hated your dream job, Cate?*
Cate *I have no idea what I'd do.*
Enzo *I know what **I** would do. I'd quit immediately. Life's too short. How about **you**?*

A 4.20 Listen and repeat the conversation. Notice how *I* and *you* are sometimes stressed to make clear who you are talking about. Then practice and continue the conversation with a partner.

B Group work Discuss the questions. Stress *I* and *you* if you need to.

- What's the best way to choose a career?
- What have some of your friends done to find work?
- What can you do if you can't decide on a career?

1 Building vocabulary and grammar

A 4.21 **Listen and read the interviews. What career plans do these students have?**

Where do you think you'll be working five years from now?

Well, I'll have finished my degree in media studies by then, and what I really want to do is get a job in **communications.** You won't be seeing me on TV or anything – I'm not cut out for that – but I may be working in, like, **publishing** or **journalism** as an **editor** or writer or something. Or maybe I'll have gotten a job in **advertising** or **public relations.** That would be fun. – Ashley

Well, in two years, I'll be graduating with a degree in **nursing** – so I'll be working in the field of **health care.** One thing I think I'd like to do is be a **psychiatric nurse,** but I'm not sure. Hopefully my wife will have graduated from medical school by then, too. She'd like to be a **pediatrician** . . . or else a **surgeon.** – Albert

I won't be doing what I'm doing now – **telemarketing** – that's for sure! This fall, I'll be starting a degree in **business management,** so in five years, I'll have graduated and gotten a job in the **construction industry.** I probably won't have had much experience, but I'll be working with **civil engineers, contractors, construction workers,** and so on. – Jesse

Hopefully I'll be working as a **financial analyst** in an investment bank. My dad's a **stockbroker,** and my mom's a **tax adviser,** so I guess I'm following them into the **financial sector.** – Simone

I don't really know. I just hope I'll be using my languages. I might be working as an **interpreter** or a **translator** – or maybe I'll be working in the **travel industry.** – Cheryl

Word sort **B** **Make a word web for each area of work. Add more jobs. Then compare with a partner. Which jobs do you think would be interesting? fun? well paid? rewarding?**

Construction industry	Medicine and health care
Financial services	Travel industry
Media and communications	Sales and marketing

civil engineer

Construction industry - architect

Figure it out **C** **Can you make these sentences true by changing the underlined words? Compare with a partner.**

Vocabulary notebook p. 126

1. Jesse will be working in telemarketing in five years.
2. In two years, Albert won't be graduating with a degree in nursing.
3. Cheryl will be working as a translator five years from now.
4. Five years from now, Ashley will be studying for her degree in media studies.

2 Grammar The future continuous and future perfect 4.22

Extra practice p. 151

Use the future continuous for ongoing activities in the future.
I'**ll be working** in health care.
I **won't be working** in this job.

Also use it for events you expect to happen.
I'**ll be graduating** in two years.
I'**ll be starting** a degree this fall.

You can use *might* and *may* instead of *will*.
I **may be working** in publishing.

Use the future perfect for events that are in the past when you "view" them from the future.
My wife **will have graduated** by then.
I probably **won't have had** much experience.

In conversation
The future continuous is much more common than the future perfect.

A **Complete the conversations using the future continuous or future perfect. Then practice with a partner.**

1. A What do you think you'll ____________ (do) five years from now?
   B I hope I'll ____________ (work) as an architect. I'll ____________ (finish) all the exams by then. How about you?
   A Well, by then I'll ____________ (graduate), too – I hope to finish my nursing degree in two years. I might ____________ (work) in a medical practice.

2. A Do you have any idea what your life will be like in ten years?
   B Well, I hope I'll ____________ (enjoy) life. I think my boyfriend and I will ____________ (get) married by then, and maybe we'll ____________ (buy) our own home. I'm not sure if we'll ____________ (start) a family, but if we have kids, I think I'll ____________ (take) care of them, and I may ____________ (work) part-time, too.

3. A What do you think you'll ____________ (do) when you're 60?
   B Well, I probably won't ____________ (stop) working, but I hope I won't ____________ (work) long hours every day.
   A Me too. Maybe by then I'll ____________ (retired), and I'll ____________ (live) by the ocean.

4. A What kinds of jobs do you think people will ____________ (do) 20 years from now?
   B I think more people will ____________ (work) in health care because people will ____________ (live) longer. Also the retirement age will ____________ (rise), too, so people might still ____________ (work) when they're 70.

About you **B** **Pair work** **Ask and answer the questions. Give your own answers. Do you have similar hopes and dreams?**

Common errors
When you are making arrangements, use the future continuous to announce your intentions.
*See you at 6. **I'll be waiting** for you in the lobby.* OR ***I'll wait** . . .* (NOT ~~*I'm waiting*~~ . . .)

3 Talk about it Working lives

Group work **Discuss the statements. Do you agree with them?**

Ten years from now, . . .

- more people will be working from home.
- fewer people will have had a college education.
- people will be retiring at a younger age.
- people will still be learning English to help them with their careers.
- the working day will have become shorter.

Sounds right p. 139

The best part was . . .

1 Conversation strategy Introducing what you say

A What kinds of summer jobs do students do? Make a list.

B 4.23 Listen to Jin-ho and Jenn. What does Jenn say about working at the theme park?

Jin-ho Didn't you work in that theme park last summer?

Jenn Yeah. In the ticket booth for the concert arena.

Jin-ho Really? How was it? The reason I ask is I was wondering about applying for a job there myself

Jenn It was good. I mean, the best part was that I got to go on all the rides for free. I don't know if you know, but you get a free season pass.

Jin-ho Cool.

Jenn Yeah. And what I thought was really good was I got to see a lot of the concerts and meet some o the performers backstage.

Jin-ho Great. Now, what I heard was that it's hard to get a job there.

Jenn Well, yeah. What I was going to tell you was that they have a job fair in the spring. I don't know if you're familiar with one, but you go around the park and interview for different jobs.

Jin-ho Yeah? Maybe I should go to that.

C Notice how Jin-ho and Jenn introduce what they say with expressions like these. Find the expressions they use.

What I thought was good was (that) . . .
The best part is / was (that) . . .
What I heard / read was (that) . . .
The reason I ask is (that) . . .
What I was going to tell you / say was (that) . . .

D 4.24 Listen. Write the expressions Jin-ho and Jenn use. Then practice.

1. **Jenn** Have you had any experience? ____________ it helps when you have previous work experience
   Jin-ho Actually, yeah. I worked in a restaurant one time. ____________ I got good tips.
2. **Jin-ho** So what will you be doing during summer break?
   Jenn I'll be working as a camp counselor this year. My friend did it last year. She said it was great. ____________ she got to go rafting and everything with the kids *and* she got paid for it.
3. **Jin-ho** How old were you when you got your first job? ____________ my sister wants to work, but she's only 15.
   Jenn ____________ you have to be 16 before you can get a job. But I'm not sure.

About you **E Pair work** Discuss the questions above. Give your own answers. Introduce what you say with expressions from the box.

2 Strategy plus *I don't know if . . .*

I don't know if . . .
can introduce a statement, often to involve the other person in the topic.

In conversation

Some of the most common expressions with ***I don't know if*** are:

I don't know if you've (ever) heard . . .
I don't know if you're familiar with . . .
I don't know if you've (ever) seen . . .

A Rewrite the sentences. Use *I don't know if* to introduce the topics.

1. Have you ever worked in a restaurant? It's really hard work.
   I don't know if you've ever worked in a restaurant, but it's really hard work.
2. Have you ever sent out your résumé? Often companies don't bother to reply.
3. Have you read about this? One of the most popular careers is engineering.
4. Do you know? The main thing employers want is reliable workers.
5. Have you heard? More and more people work while they're on vacation.
6. Are you familiar with all those jobs websites? You can post your résumé on them.
7. Did you read? 80% of people are not satisfied with their jobs.
8. Have you heard this? On average, people in the U.S. change jobs seven times before they turn 30.

B Pair work Take turns saying the sentences to start conversations.

3 Listening and strategies An interesting job

A 4.25 Can you answer any of the questions below? Then listen to a personal trainer talk about her work. Which questions does she answer? Check (✓) the questions.

- ☐ What is a personal trainer's main role?
- ☐ Why do people hire personal trainers?
- ☐ How do you become a personal trainer?
- ☐ Is a personal trainer's job rewarding? Why?
- ☐ Are all trainers certified?
- ☐ What are the disadvantages of the job?
- ☐ How much do personal trainers earn?
- ☐ How do you find a good trainer?

B 4.25 Listen again. How does the personal trainer answer the questions? Write two pieces of information for each question.

About you **C Group work Discuss the questions.**

- What's the most unusual or interesting job you've heard about?
- What jobs do people you know have? Which is the most challenging? Why?
- Are there any jobs that you really wouldn't want to do? Why not?
- What's the first job you ever did? Was it fun?
- What would be an exciting job? Why?

"Well, I don't know if you've ever seen the work of an interior designer, but they seem to have a really interesting job. What I heard was . . . "

1 Reading

A What would you do to prepare for a job interview? Make a class list.

"One thing you need to do is research the company."

B Look at the three interview questions in the article. How would you answer them? Compare your ideas with a partner. Then read the article. How would you change your answers?

Reading tip

Try to predict the "great answers" to the questions before you read them.

Ace that Interview!

Tough Questions, Great Answers

Nothing can trip you up during an interview like an unexpected or difficult question. Whether you're applying for an internship, trying to get into college, or interviewing for a new job, here are a few questions that might stump you – along with the kinds of answers interviewers like to hear.

"Tell me about yourself."

Be ready to describe what makes you special as an individual. "What I *don't* want to hear is your life history," explains Dennis B., Director of Admissions at a major university. "I don't care how many siblings you have or where you were born. I want to know what makes you special. I want to see how well you project yourself, if you're articulate, and to hear your reasons for applying to do this course of study." The same applies at a job interview. Be concise and give concrete examples: "The main thing you should know about me is that while I was in college, I had a side job retrieving lost data from computers. I set up and marketed the business myself. I had 80 customers in the first year."

"What draws you to this line of work?"

Know what you're getting yourself into. "Publishing is a tough profession," says Tracy P., Editorial Director at a publishing house in New York City. "Unfortunately, some people want to get into it for the wrong reasons. Many candidates mention how much they love books and reading. However, that doesn't necessarily mean that editing or the business side of publishing is a good profession for you. You might be better suited to teaching, for example. If someone doesn't understand the profession, the chances are they won't be a good fit for this type of work." In other words, show that you understand what the job involves in your response to the question and give an example of how you have acquired the relevant skills: "One skill you need to work in publishing is attention to detail. I worked on the college magazine and edited articles . . . "

"Tell me about a time you made a serious mistake. How did you handle it?"

"Many of our candidates get hired right after they graduate from college, before they've had a chance to get much work experience," notes Anita M., head of recruiting at a Fortune 500 financial company. "The reason I ask this question is that it's a tough question for everybody, and how a person answers is very revealing. It's important that people admit when they've made a mistake, rather than blame others. What I'm saying is that I expect candidates to be honest, and I look for signs that they've learned from the mistake." So, don't say you have never really made a mistake. Instead, try something along these lines: "One thing I did while I was working on a project in college was let down my team. I didn't complete my part of the project on time. I apologized. I also explained to the professor it was my fault and asked for an extension. Then I made it up to my teammates by working all weekend to finish the project. It taught me how to manage my time and not leave things until the last minute."

Remember: Speak clearly and at a normal pace of conversation. Don't rush your words because you're nervous. Be calm and speak with confidence.

C Pair work Discuss your answers to the questions below.

1. What trips up some candidates during an interview, according to the article?
2. What mistake do some candidates make when they are asked to talk about themselves?
3. What two things do you need to tell an interviewer to show you're right for the job?
4. Why is it revealing when candidates talk about mistakes they have made?
5. Which question do you think is the most difficult one to answer? Why?

2 Listening and writing A fabulous opportunity!

A 4.26 Read the online job advertisement. Can you guess the missing words? Then listen to Maria talk about the ad with her friend Alex. Were any of your guesses correct?

Job summary

Company

____

Location

Montreal

Job type

- ● Part-time
- ○ Full-time

Tour Guide

A leading tour company is seeking someone who would enjoy meeting ______________ from other countries. You must be fluent in ______________ and ______________. You should be interested in the local area and its ______________. You'll be traveling around the region ______________ days a week. Flexible, fun, and ______________ applicants only.

Apply by email, and also send your ______________. Successful applicants will receive excellent pay and a generous benefits package.

APPLY

B 4.26 Listen again. Why is Maria perfect for this job? Write four reasons.

C Imagine you want to apply for the job above. Read the Help note and write a cover letter like the one below.

You are applying for: **Tour Guide**
- Upload a résumé
- Include a cover letter

SUBMIT

Dear Sir or Madam,

I am applying for the position of Tour Guide, which was advertised on April 1. My strongest qualification for this position is that I speak fluent English and Spanish.

As you can see from the attached résumé, I have had previous experience in this type of work with students from abroad who attend summer programs. It was my responsibility to show them around campus and the local area. In addition, I have . . .

I am enthusiastic about this opportunity as I am considering a career in the tourist industry. I believe that I would be an excellent guide and that tour groups would appreciate my knowledge of the region, my sense of humor, and positive attitude.

I would welcome the opportunity to meet with you. My contact number is 917-555-1954. Thank you for your time and consideration.

Sincerely,
Sergei Vnukov

Help note

Writing a cover letter

- Use the name of the person if you can. If you don't know it, use *Sir or Madam*.
- Opening paragraph: State what the position is, how you heard about it, and what your strongest qualification for it is.
- Middle paragraph(s): Say why you are suitable – give more information about your qualifications or experience, and describe your strengths.
- Closing paragraph: Restate your interest and offer to meet for an interview. Thank the person for his or her time.
- End the letter like this.

D **Group work** Read your classmates' cover letters. Who do you think should get the job?

Free talk p. 136

Vocabulary notebook From accountant to zoologist

Learning tip *Word building with roots and collocations*

When you learn a new word, you can expand your vocabulary quickly by learning

- other words with the same root.
- some common collocations.

journalism *journalist*

political journalist *freelance journalist*

In conversation

Teachers are tops!

The job people talk about most is ***teacher***.

1 Complete the chart with the areas of work and the jobs.

Area of work	Job
accounting	accountant
architecture	
	carpenter
counseling	
	dentist
design	
editing	
	engineer
financial analysis	

Area of work	Job
	interpreter
law	
	manager
	nurse
pediatrics	
	photographer
physical therapy	
	plumber

Area of work	Job
psychiatry	
	psychologist
	publisher
sales	
	surgeon
telemarketing	
	translator
	zoologist

2 Word builder Match the words in A with the words in B to make common collocations. How many jobs can you make? Can you add any more words to make different job combinations?

A	
civil	psychiatric
construction	social
laboratory	systems
pediatric	

B	
analyst	technician
engineer	worker
nurse	

On your own

Find a jobs website. Write the names of 20 different jobs in English.

Can Do! Now I can . . .

✓ I can . . .   ? I need to review how to . . .

- ☐ talk about career planning.
- ☐ highlight important information.
- ☐ talk about professions and job prospects.
- ☐ talk about my future career plans.
- ☐ use expressions to introduce what I say.
- ☐ say *I don't know if* . . . to involve others.
- ☐ understand a conversation with a personal trainer.
- ☐ understand a discussion about a job advertisement.
- ☐ read an article about preparing for a job interview.
- ☐ write a cover letter for a job application.

1 Talking about jobs

Match the two parts of each sentence. Then discuss them with a partner. Add ideas and expressions like *and so on*, *and so forth*, and *etc.*

1. Being a surgeon is very rewarding, __c__
2. Stockbrokers are under a lot of stress ____
3. It's easy to get health-care jobs these days ____
4. Workers are being brought into the country ____
5. Plan your career in five-year blocks ____
6. More students are taking media studies, ____
7. There are fewer telemarketing jobs ____

a. even though really good jobs are hard to get.
b. in order to fill all the jobs in construction.
c. in spite of the long hours you have to work.
d. so that you can set realistic goals.
e. because of the shortage of nurses.
f. as a result of outsourcing to other countries.
g. due to the constant changes in financial markets.

"I imagine being a surgeon is rewarding, in spite of the long hours and the stress and so on."

2 How many words can you think of?

A Add six words and expressions to each category, and compare with a partner.

Being famous	
in the headlines	

The environment	

B Pair work Choose four items from each category to use in a conversation. How many different expressions can you remember to introduce what you say?

A *I don't know if you've heard, but Angelina Jolie is in the headlines right now.*
B *Oh, yeah. What I heard was she recently . . .*

3 What will life be like in 2030?

A Complete the sentences using the future continuous or future perfect.

1. Hopefully, by 2030, people __*will be buying*__ (buy) more and more environmentally friendly products, and we ________ (find) new ways to save energy, so we ________ (live) in a cleaner environment.
2. Ideally, we ________ (slow) global warming by then. We ________ (not use) fuels like coal anymore. More countries ________ (start) to use cleaner, more efficient fuels.
3. By 2030, people ________ (eat) healthier food, and the number of obese people ________ (decrease).
4. Because we ________ (live) longer, the percentage of older people in society ________ (rise) by then.

B Group work Discuss the sentences. Refer back to what people say with expressions like *As you said*, *Like you were saying*, and *Going back to . . . .* Add your opinions.

4 What if . . . ?

"I applied for an internship at a public relations company after college. At the end of my interview, they offered me a job. Now, 20 years later, I'm still there, and I'm vice president."
– Alice

"I was bored with my job at the bank, so I saw a career counselor and took some personality tests. They showed I was creative! So I went into advertising, and I love it."
– Martin

"I was going to major in math at college, but I got sick the first week and had to drop out. In the hospital, I got interested in nursing, and so now, here I am – a pediatric nurse."
– Alfonso

A **Read the comments above. How might these people's lives have been different? Write sentences using *if* + the past perfect form and *would have, could have,* or *may / might have*.**

If Alice hadn't applied for an internship at that company, she wouldn't have ended up working there.

B **Pair work Talk about three big decisions you've made in life. Ask and answer hypothetical questions. If a question is difficult to answer, use an expression like *Good question*.**

5 Check it out.

What do you know about your partner? Complete the sentences, adding tag questions. Then ask your partner.

1. You live in ____________, *don't you*?
2. You've studied English for ____________ years, ____________?
3. You don't like ____________ music, ____________?
4. You're a ____________, ____________?
5. You went to ____________ on vacation once, ____________?

6 Any suggestions?

Complete the sentences using the passive of the present continuous or present perfect. Then role-play with a partner. Take turns making suggestions.

1. "We *'re being given* (give) too much homework these days."
2. "I ____________ (ask) to do volunteer work, but I'm too busy."
3. "I ____________ (promote) at work, but I prefer my old job!"
4. "People ____________ (lay off) at work recently. I'm worried because I ____________ (pay) more than my co-workers."

A ***We're being given too much homework these days.***
B ***You could talk to your teacher about it, couldn't you?***

UNIT 7 Who gets help with something?

Class activity Ask and answer the questions. Find someone who answers yes. Ask questions to find out more information.

Do you know anyone who . . .

- gets family photos taken professionally?
- got someone to run an errand for them recently?
- has something at home that needs to be fixed?
- is having their house decorated?
- often gets a friend to help with homework?
- likes to get pizza delivered at home?
- got a tech center to solve a computer problem recently?
- owns something that is old and needs replacing?

UNIT 8 How did you react?

1 Think of a time an incident happened to you. Use the ideas below or one of your own.

something went wrong with a cab ride	someone got mad at you
you yelled at someone	you had to get out of a date or appointment
you were late for something	someone was rude to you

2 Prepare your story about the incident to tell the group. What happened? How did you react? How did the people around you react? Think of as many details as you can.

3 **Group work** Take turns telling your stories. Listen to your classmates' stories. Ask questions. Think about what happened and say why. Have you had a similar thing happen to you? Tell the group.

So one time, I was driving with my friend, and this car was behind us, and the driver was trying to get past us. And he kept honking and flashing his lights. And my friend got really mad and called the police on his cell phone . . .

The driver behind you must have been in a hurry. He could have been on his way to the hospital.

Yeah, but he shouldn't have driven like that. It's dangerous.

I had something like that happen to me one time. . . .

UNIT 10 Quotations

1 **Group work** Look at the quotations below. Do you agree with them? Which one is your favorite?

A man is a success if he gets up in the morning and gets to bed at night, and in between does what he wants to do. – Bob Dylan

Having a lot of money does not automatically make you a successful person. What you want is money and meaning. You want your work to be meaningful, because meaning is what brings the real richness to your life. – Oprah Winfrey

You don't have to be famous. You just have to make your mother and father proud of you. – Meryl Streep

Success is a state of mind. If you want success, start thinking of yourself as a success. – Dr. Joyce Brothers

All you need in this life is ignorance and confidence; then success is sure. – Mark Twain

Success is really about being ready for the good opportunities that come before you. – Eric Schmidt

2 Can you think up your own definition of "success"? Complete the sentence below.

Success is ______________________________ .

3 **Class activity** Now go around the class and find out your classmates' definitions. Choose the two you like best, and write them down with your classmates' names. Then share your new "quotations" with the class.

UNIT 9

Material things

1 **Complete the questions below with your own ideas on the topic of "material things."**

Material things

1. Can you imagine life without ______________________________?
2. How many ______________________________ do you own?
3. Have you ever bought ______________________________?
4. Are you good at ______________________________?
5. ______________________________ money?
6. When did you last ______________________________?
7. Do you think you'll ever own a ______________________________?
8. Do you think people ______________________________?

2 **Pair work** **Ask and answer your questions. Remember the questions your partner asks.**

3 **Pair work** **Find a new partner. Tell each other the questions you were asked, and say how you answered them.**

"Mario asked me if I could imagine life without the Internet. I told him I had to go without the Internet las weekend, and it was awful!"

UNIT 11 What's trending?

1 **Pair work** Look at the topics below. What trends have you noticed in each of these areas? Brainstorm ideas and make a list.

education
online learning and webinars
more testing

2 **Group work** Join another pair. Discuss the trends on your list. What are they a result of? What impact do you think they will have? Can you predict any trends for the future in these areas?

A *Well, online learning is definitely being introduced into schools in this area.*
B *It's interesting, don't you think? I mean, why is that?*
C *I think it's a result of the demand for more flexible learning opportunities.*

UNIT 12 The best person for the job

1 **Look at the different jobs below. Choose a job that you'd like to apply for, and prepare for a job interview. Think of answers to the following questions.**

- Why are you interested in this job?
- What experience and qualifications do you have?
- What are your main strengths and weaknesses?
- What qualities do you think someone needs to do this job well?
- Where do you see yourself in five years?

2 **Group work** "Interview" each person for the job they want to apply for. Take turns asking the questions above. At the end of the interview, hold a group vote, and decide if the person should be hired.

"So, Amelie, why are you interested in a job as a student counselor?"

Sounds right

UNIT 7 4.33 Listen and repeat the words. Notice the underlined sounds. Are the sounds like the sounds in *enjoy*, *choose*, *done*, *serviced*, *straight*, or *there*? Write the words from the list in the correct columns below.

1. adjust
2. curtains
3. decorate
4. emergency
5. flooded
6. hair
7. noise
8. oil
9. paint
10. repair
11. routine
12. screwdriver

enjoy	choose	done	serviced	straight	there
		adjust			

UNIT 8 4.34 Listen and repeat the pairs of words. Notice the underlined sounds. Are the sounds the same (S) or different (D)? Write *S* or *D*.

1. stressed / dead *S*
2. emotional / gotten ____
3. aggressive / angry ____
4. jealous / intelligent ____
5. should / motivation ____
6. decisive / discipline ____
7. aggression / depressed ____
8. sympathetic / guilty ____
9. confidence / honesty ____

UNIT 9

4.35 **Listen and repeat the words. Underline the silent letter in each word.**

1. answer
2. budget
3. debt
4. gadget
5. honest
6. should
7. sign
8. walk
9. could
10. might
11. half
12. listen

UNIT 10

4.36 **Listen and repeat the words. Notice that one or more syllables in each word are unstressed. They have a weak vowel which sounds like the /ə/ sound in *person*. Circle the weak vowels.**

1. album
2. amazing
3. career
4. confidence
5. connections
6. extra
7. famous
8. happened
9. millionaire
10. recently
11. seminar
12. talent

UNIT 11

4.37 **Listen and repeat the words. Notice the underlined sounds. Which sound in each group is different? Circle the word with the sound that's different.**

1.	consumption	natural	ocean	shortage
2.	congestion	energy	garbage	gas
3.	conserve	consume	recycle	rising
4.	carbon	outsource	warming	warning
5.	change	chemical	packaging	technology
6.	because	brought	drought	talk

UNIT 12

4.38 **Listen and repeat the words. Notice the underlined sounds. Are the sounds like the sounds in *analyst*, *apply*, *construction*, *engineer*, *personality*, or *recruit*? Write the words from the list in the correct columns below.**

1. advertising
2. business
3. choose
4. career
5. civil
6. love
7. experience
8. psychiatric
9. publishing
10. research
11. surgeon
12. school

analyst	apply	construction	engineer	personality	recruit
	advertising				

Extra practice

UNIT 7

Lesson A Causative *get* and *have*

A Complete the sentences. Use the verbs given.

1. I don't have my clothes *cleaned* (clean) professionally.
2. We usually have my brother ____________ (repair) things around the house.
3. My friends get me ____________ (fix) their computer problems.
4. I've never had my hair ____________ (color).
5. I often get my sister ____________ (cook) for me.
6. My neighbor gets his windows ____________ (wash) every week.
7. When I throw a party, I get friends ____________ (help) me.
8. I don't have my car ____________ (service) regularly.
9. I always get people ____________ (help) me when I try to fix anything in the house.
10. I don't buy new shoes very often. I like to get them ____________ (repair). In fact, I'm having a pair of boots ____________ (repair) right now.

About you **B Pair work Are the sentences above true for you? How do you get these things done? Discuss with a partner.**

UNIT 7

Lesson B *need* + passive infinitive and *need* + verb + *-ing*

A Complete the list of things that need doing in Mia's apartment.

- *front door doesn't close – fix the lock*
- *some lights don't work – change the bulbs*
- *large crack in window – replace the glass*
- *shelves in kitchen aren't straight – adjust them*
- *TV making a strange noise – repair it*
- *leaking bathroom faucet – tighten the faucet*
- *dirty rug – clean it*
- *stain on kitchen wall – paint it*

1. The lock needs *to be fixed / fixing* .
2. Some bulbs need ____________________ .
3. The glass in the window needs ____________________ .
4. The shelves need ____________________ .
5. The TV needs ____________________ .
6. The faucet needs ____________________ .
7. The rug needs ____________________ .
8. The wall needs ____________________ .

In conversation

need + passive infinitive is more common than ***need*** + verb + *-ing*.

need + verb + *-ing*

need + passive infinitive

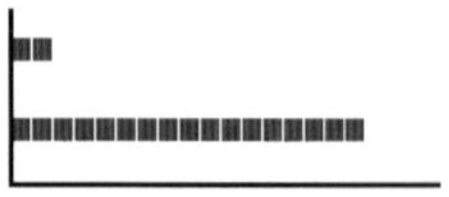

About you **B Pair work Do any of the things above need doing in your apartment? Tell a partner. What else needs fixing?**

UNIT 8

Lesson A Past modals *would have, should have, could have*

A ~~Cross out~~ the incorrect words. Then write answers to the questions.

1. Dan's daughter was sick and couldn't go to school. Dan took her to work with him. What could / ~~would~~ he have done instead? ______________________
2. Ashley had a meal at a restaurant. The food was tasteless, and the service was rude. She complained politely and left. What else could / would she have done? ______________________
3. There were six cartons of milk left at the grocery store. A man pushed in front of me and picked up all six. I really needed one. Should / Would I have said something? ______________________
4. Sara borrowed a dress of Kate's. She spilled coffee on it. She gave it back with a stain on it without saying anything. What should / would she have done? ______________________
5. Josh bought a camera. It should have cost $500, but the salesperson charged him the wrong price of $395. Should / Would Josh have said anything? ______________________
6. Hal had an important meeting that he hadn't prepared for. He said he wasn't feeling well and went home. Would / Should you have done the same thing? ______________________

About you **B Pair work Discuss your answers to the questions above. Do you have the same views?**

Common errors

Use *should have*, not *must have*, + past participle, to talk about the right thing to do.

*She **should have** called me.* (NOT ~~*She must have called me*~~.)

UNIT 8

Lesson B Past modals for speculation

A Write a sentence to explain each situation. Start the sentences with the words given. There may be more than one correct answer.

1. You're stuck in a traffic jam, and you're sure there's been an accident.
   "There *must have been an accident* ______________________."
2. You're in a nice restaurant, and the couple at the table next to you aren't talking to each other. You think it's possible they've had a fight.
   "They ______________________."
3. You don't think it's possible that you left your credit card at the store.
   "I ______________________."
4. When you arrive at the dentist for an appointment, they tell you that you are an hour late. You think it's possible you wrote down the wrong time.
   "I ______________________."
5. You call your sister, but someone else answers. You're sure that you called the wrong number.
   "I ______________________."
6. Your mother didn't send you a birthday card. It's not possible that she has forgotten.
   "She ______________________."

About you **B Pair work Compare your answers. Have you ever been in situations like the ones above? Share stories.**

C Pair work Imagine that you're at a coffee shop. You can't find your wallet to pay. Think of as many reasons as you can why this is possible. Tell your partner.

"I must have left my wallet at home."

Extra practice

UNIT 9 Lesson A Reported speech

> **Note**
>
> Present continuous forms in direct speech shift back to past continuous forms in reported speech.
>
> *"I'm **destroying** all my things."*
> *→ He said that he **was destroying** all his things.*

A Read what Pablo says. Then complete the sentences to report what he said.

"I don't think that I'm very materialistic. I'm moving to a new apartment soon, and so I've been trying to get rid of the things I don't want. I actually think I'm very self-disciplined – I only spend money on things I really need. I mean, I've kept a few gifts that I've never used. You know, things that close friends gave to me. And I've kept some old family photos that I can't throw away, obviously. But over the years, I've bought a lot of books, and I'll probably give most of them away."

1. Pablo said that he *didn't think* that he ____________ very materialistic.
2. He said he ____________ to a new apartment, and so he ____________ to get rid of the things he ____________ .
3. He said he ____________ that he ____________ very self-disciplined and said he only ____________ money on things he really ____________ .
4. He said that he ____________ a few gifts that he ____________ ____________ – things that close friends ____________ to him.
5. He said he ____________ some old family photos that he ____________ throw away.
6. He said that over the years, he ____________ a lot of books and that he ____________ probably give most of them away.

> **Common errors**
>
> Don't use *say* + *me*, *him*, *them*, etc.
>
> *She said she wasn't materialistic.*
> (NOT ~~*She said me she wasn't materialistic.*~~)

About you **B Pair work** **Ask your partner, "Are you materialistic? Could you give away your possessions?" Then find another partner and report the answers.**

UNIT 9 Lesson B Reported questions

A Imagine a market researcher asked you these questions. Write the reported questions.

1. Are you saving up for anything special? *He asked me if . . .*
2. How much money have you spent today?
3. What's your favorite store?
4. Could you live without your smartphone?
5. How do you keep track of your money?
6. Does your bank account pay good interest?
7. How often do you check your bank account?
8. Do you ever spend too much on things?

> **In conversation**
>
> *. . . asked **if*** and *. . . wanted to know **if*** are much more frequent than *. . . asked **whether*** and *. . . wanted to know **whether**.*

> **Common errors**
>
> Don't use *tell* to report questions.
>
> *She **asked** me if I owned any stocks.*
> (NOT ~~*She told me if I owned any stocks.*~~)

About you **B Pair work** **Ask and answer the questions. Then find another partner and report the questions and your first partner's answers.**

UNIT 10

Lesson A Talking hypothetically about the past

A These people are talking hypothetically about the past. Complete the sentences.

1. If I _had worked_ (work) harder at school, I might have gotten a better job.
2. If I hadn't quit my job, I ____________ (would not meet) my new friends.
3. If my family ____________ (not encourage) me, I wouldn't have had the confidence to apply for my current job.
4. If my neighbor ____________ (take) different subjects, he would have had better job opportunities.
5. If I'd gotten better grades, I ____________ (could get) into grad school.
6. If I had studied English at an earlier age, I ____________ (might take) this class years ago.
7. If my parents hadn't set aside the money, they ____________ (could not afford) a big house.
8. If we ____________ (grow up) 50 years ago, our lives might have been very different.

About you **B Pair work Make four of the sentences above true for you, and tell a partner. Give more information.**

"If my friend Robin had worked harder in school, she would have passed more exams and she would have gotten a better job."

UNIT 10

Lesson B Tag questions

A Complete the sentences with a tag question.

1. Celebrity couples often have problems with their marriages, _don't they_ ?
2. People are not really watching reality shows anymore, ____________ ? They've lost interest in them.
3. You don't have to have a lot of confidence to go on a talent show, ____________ ?
4. It's easier to become an Internet celebrity these days, ____________ ?
5. Some actors don't deserve all the bad press they get, ____________ ?
6. To be successful in Hollywood, you have to have connections, ____________ ?
7. Some singers are just terrible when they perform live, ____________ ? I'm not the only one who thinks that, ____________ ?
8. The old black and white movies were much better than today's movies, ____________ ?
9. Some actors have dropped out of sight completely, ____________ ?
10. They're making a lot of violent movies these days, ____________ ? I'm right about that, ____________ ?

i Note

Notice how to make tag questions when the verb in the statement is *have* or a continuous verb.

*You **have** a guitar, **don't you?***

*She **didn't have** connections, **did she?***

*He**'s doing** really well, **isn't he?***

*They **were getting** bad press, **weren't they?***

Notice how to make tag questions with *I'm . . .* and *I'm not . . .*

***I'm** right, **aren't I**?*

***I'm** not wrong, **am I**?*

About you **B Pair work Start conversations with the sentences above. Do you agree? Give your own views.**

UNIT 11

Lesson A Passive of present continuous and present perfect

A Which of the sentences below need a passive, not an active, verb? Correct the sentences.

1. Fewer jobs are ~~creating~~ *being created* in the construction industry.
2. Fast food chains are providing healthier meals.
3. Skilled workers have recruited from other countries.
4. Smoking has banned in public places.
5. A lot of older houses have knocked down to make room for new buildings.
6. In the last few years, young people haven't encouraged to go to college.
7. Plans to address water shortages have not discussed.
8. More and more life-saving medicines have developed in the last ten years.
9. A large number of bank employees have laid off because their jobs have outsourced to other countries.
10. New gyms and swimming pools are building in some neighborhoods because people are demanding better facilities.

Common errors

Don't forget to use the passive when you don't know who is doing the action.

More roads ***are being built*** *every year.* (NOT ~~*More roads are building every year.*~~)

About you **B Pair work Which of the sentences above are true where you live? Discuss with a partner.**

UNIT 11

Lesson B Linking ideas

A Rewrite the sentences using the expressions given.

1. I think it's better to get around by bicycle than to drive your car everywhere. (instead of)
   I think it's better to get around by bicycle instead of driving your car everywhere.
2. I'm concerned that carbon dioxide levels are rising because of increased burning of fuels. (due to)
   ______
3. I'm worried that congestion on the roads is still a problem, even though there have been improvements. (in spite of)
   ______
4. It's annoying that people often throw away plastic bottles when you can recycle them. (even though)
   ______
5. I think we should use things like lemon juice as a cleaning product – then we won't need to buy so many toxic chemicals. (so that)
   ______
6. We should reduce our energy use so we can protect the environment. (in order to)
   ______
7. It worries me that obesity in children is becoming more of a problem because of unhealthy eating habits. (as a result of)
   ______

About you **B Pair work Do you agree with any of the concerns above? Brainstorm solutions to the problems.**

UNIT 12 Lesson A *What* clauses and long noun phrases as subjects

A Rewrite these sentences to give someone advice about starting a new job. Start with the words given.

1. Making a good impression is really important.
   What ______________________________.
2. A friend of mine offered to help the manager.
   Something ______________________________.
3. My sister introduced herself to everyone.
   What ______________________________.
4. Smile – that's the best thing you can do.
   The ______________________________.
5. I would try to listen and learn from your co-workers.
   What ______________________________.
6. I like to find out as much about the job as possible before starting. Then you feel prepared.
   What ______________________________.
   The advantage of that ______________________________.

About you **B Pair work Do you agree with this advice? What other advice do you have for someone on their first day at work?**

UNIT 12 Lesson B The future continuous and future perfect

A Read what Natalie says about her future. Then complete the sentences.

"I'm finishing my degree in math right now. I hope I do well on my exams because I've applied to go to medical school next year. The program lasts four years, and then there are three to seven years of internship to do after that. I don't know what type of medicine I want to work in yet, but I have a lot of time to decide. I might go and work in another country. Who knows?"

1. In a few months, Natalie __________ (finish) her degree in math, and she __________ (get) ready to go to medical school.
2. Five years after that, she __________ (leave) medical school, and she __________ (do) an internship somewhere.
3. She probably __________ (not decide) which area of medicine she'd like to work in by then.
4. She doesn't know who she __________ (work) with or where she __________ (live).
5. She __________ (might move) to a different country to work.

About you **B Pair work Think of three ideas for each question. Tell your partner.**

What will you be doing . . .

- 24 hours from now?
- in three months?
- in five years?

What will you have done by then?

Illustration credits

Harry Briggs: 7, 31, 55, 68, 69, 95 **Bunky Hurter:** 14, 36, 54, 77, 100 **Scott Macneil:** 71 **Q2A studio artists:** 24, 47, 57, 79, 89 **Lucy Truman:** 10, 20, 30, 42, 52, 62, 74, 84, 94, 106, 116, 126

Photography credits

Back cover: ©vovan/Shutterstock **38, 39, 58, 59, 90, 91, 112, 113** ©Cambridge University Press **6, 7, 12, 26, 27, 70, 71, 80, 102, 103, 118, 122, 123** ©Frank Veronsky **viii** *(left to right) ©RubberBall/SuperStock; ©Cultura Limited/SuperStock* **1** *(clockwise from top left)* ©Marmaduke St. John/Alamy; ©Exactostock/SuperStock; ©Nicola Tree/Getty Images; ©Steven Robertson/istockphoto **2** ©Thinkstock; *(top background)* ©monticello/Shutterstock **3** ©Masterfile/RF **4** ©blackred/istockphoto; *(background)* ©ruskpp/Shutterstock **8** ©Jordan Strauss/Invision/AP; *(utensils)* ©Martin Kemp/Shutterstock **9** ©2010 AFP/Getty Images **11** *(clockwise from top left)* ©Blend Images/SuperStock; ©Radius/SuperStock; ©Transtock/SuperStock; ©Blend Images/SuperStock **12** *(all photos)* ©Frank Veronsky **13** ©Thomas Barwick/Getty Images **15** *(all photos)* ©Cambridge University Press **16** ©Imagemore/SuperStock **17** ©Imagemore/SuperStock **18** *(left to right)* ©quavondo/Getty Images; ©Dreampictures/Media Bakery **21** *(clockwise from top left)* ©Pixtal/SuperStock; ©miker/Shutterstock.com; ©Pixtal/SuperStock; ©Steve Vidler/SuperStock; ©Pacific Stock - Design Pics/SuperStock; ©windmoon/Shutterstock.com **22** *(clockwise from top left)* ©Gregory Johnston/age fotostock/SuperStock; ©Linzy Slusher/istockphoto; ©Thinkstock; ©Juanmonino/Getty Images; ©Thinkstock; ©Kerrie Kerr/istockphoto; ©Steve Kaufman/CORBIS; ©Marco Maccarini/istockphoto **25** ©Bill Sykes Images/Getty Images **28** *(background)* ©Shutterstock **29** *(all backgrounds)* ©Shutterstock **32** *(top to bottom)* ©Blend Images/SuperStock; ©4kodiak/istockphoto **33** *(clockwise from top left)* ©Chris Whitehead/Getty Images; ©Thinkstock; ©Thinkstock; ©PYMCA/SuperStock **34** *(clockwise from top left)* ©Thinkstock; ©Fancy Collection/SuperStock; ©Thinkstock; ©Jupiterimages/Thinkstock; ©Edward Bock/istockphoto; ©Mie Ahmt/istockphoto; ©Exactostock/SuperStock; ©Silvia Jansen/istockphoto **35** ©Image Source/SuperStock **40** *(hole)* ©Fotana/Shutterstock **41** ©Nicole S. Young/istockphoto **43** *(clockwise from top right)* ©Transtock/SuperStock; ©Thinkstock; ©Exactostock/SuperStock **44** *(clockwise from top left)* ©Thinkstock; ©Thinkstock; ©Jupiterimages/Thinkstock; ©Jupiterimages/Thinkstock; ©Thinkstock **48** *(people)* ©Blaj Gabriel/Shutterstock *(bus stop)* ©Joy Rector/Shutterstock *(sign)* ©Rob Wilson/Shutterstock **49** *(top)* ©Blaj Gabriel/Shutterstock *(bottom)* ©Jack Hollingsworth/Getty Images **50** ©Olivier Lantzendörffer/istockphoto; *(background)* ©Hluboki Dzianis/Shutterstock **51** *(background)* ©Hluboki Dzianis/Shutterstock **53** *(clockwise from top left)* ©The Power of Forever Photography/istockphoto; ©PhotoAlto/SuperStock; ©Thinkstock; ©Thinkstock; ©Ingram Publishing/SuperStock **54** *(left to right)* ©Paul Hakimata/Fotolia; ©Jupiterimages/Thinkstock **56** *(top section, top to bottom)* ©Eric Isselee/Shutterstock; ©Flavia Morlachetti/Shutterstock; ©Eric Isselee/Shutterstock; ©ULKASTUDIO/Shutterstock; ©Coprid/Shutterstock *(bottom row, left to right)* ©Morgan Lane Photography/Shutterstock; ©Peter Waters/Shutterstock; ©Eric Isselee/Shutterstock; ©Yu Lan/Shutterstock; (background) ©sunil menon/istockphoto **60** Photo Courtesy of Mary E. Holmes **63** *(left to right)* ©Arcady/Shutterstock; ©Arcady/Shutterstock; ©Miguel Angel Salinas Salinas/Shutterstock; ©Arcady/Shutterstock; ©Olga Anourina/istockphoto **64** ©altrendo images/Getty Images **65** *(clockwise from top left)* ©Yuri Arcurs Media/SuperStock; ©Exactostock/SuperStock; ©Niels Busch/Getty Images; ©Blend Images/SuperStock; ©baranq/Shutterstock; ©moodboard/SuperStock **66** *(clockwise from top left)* ©Michael Hitoshi/Getty Images; ©Jupiterimages/Thinkstock; ©Catherine Yeulet/istockphoto; ©Jupiterimages/Getty Images **67** *(invitation)* ©mark wragg/istockphoto *(photographer)* ©Marcin Stefaniak/istockphoto *(cake)* ©Dean Turner/istockphoto *(dress)* ©fStop/SuperStock *(flowers)* ©RubberBall/SuperStock *(passport)* ©Lana Sundman/age fotostock/SuperStock **73** ©Dfree/Shutterstock **75** *(clockwise from top left)* ©Thinkstock; ©Thinkstock; ©Thinkstock; ©Photo and Co/Getty Images **76** ©digitalskillet/istockphoto **81** ©BanksPhotos/istockphoto **82** ©Michael Rosenwirth/Alamy; *(background)* ©argus/Shutterstock **85** *(clockwise from top right)* ©Thinkstock; ©Jamie Grill/Getty Images; ©Fotosearch/SuperStock; ©Dmitry Kalinovsky/istockphoto **86** *(top, left to right)* ©WireImage/Getty Images; ©Julian Stallabrass/Flickr; *(bottom)* ©Photocrea/Shutterstock **88** *(background)* © photolinc/Shutterstock **91** ©Bruce Glikas/Getty Images **92** ©stevecoleimages/istockphoto; *(background)* ©Loskutnikov/Shutterstock **97** *(clockwise from bottom left)* ©Getty Images; ©Indigo/Getty Images; ©Getty Images; ©GYI NSEA/istockphoto; ©GYI NSEA/istockphoto **98** *(top to bottom)* ©Featureflash/Shutterstock.com; ©Thinkstock; ©Ciaran Griffin/Thinkstock; ©Comstock Images/Thinkstock; *(background)* ©Henning Riemer/Shutterstock **99** ©Paul A. Hebert/Getty Images **101** *(top to bottom)* ©Getty Images; ©Time & Life Pictures/Getty Images **104** *(left to right)* ©GYI NSEA/istockphoto; ©Featureflash/Shutterstock.com; ©GYI NSEA/istockphoto **107** *(clockwise from top left)* ©Edward Bock/istockphoto; ©TIM MCCAIG/istockphoto; ©Johner/SuperStock; ©Thinkstock **108** *(top row, left to right)* ©Thinkstock; ©Comstock Images/Thinkstock; ©Thinkstock *(bottom row, all photos)* ©Thinkstock **110** ©Thinkstock **114** *(top to bottom)* ©Debby Wong/Shutterstock.com; ©Stockbyte/Thinkstock; *(background)* ©Itana/Shutterstock **115** ©Thinkstock; *(background)* ©Itana/Shutterstock **117** *(clockwise from top left)* ©Jack Hollingsworth/Thinkstock; ©Andrew Rich/istockphoto; ©Alexander Podshivalov/istockphoto; ©Blend Images/SuperStock **120** *(clockwise from top left)* ©Thinkstock; ©ViviSuArt/istockphoto; ©Neustockimages/istockphoto; ©Don Bayley/istockphoto; ©Thinkstock **124** ©age fotostock/SuperStock **128** *(left to right)* ©Rich Legg/istockphoto; ©daniel rodriguez/istockphoto; ©Stephanie Swartz/istockphoto **130** *(left to right)* ©Martijn Mulder/istockphoto; ©Corbis/SuperStock **131** ©Oliver Gutfleisch/ima/imagebroker.net/SuperStock **132** ©Ghislain & Marie David de Lossy/Getty Images **134** ©Monkey Business Images/Shutterstock **135** *(clockwise from top left)* ©hxdbzxy/Shutterstock; ©Sandra Baker/Alamy; ©bikeriderlondon/Shutterstock; ©ArtFamily/Shutterstock **136** *(background)* ©Gunnar Pippel/Shutterstock **141** *(top to bottom)* ©Thinkstock; ©Thinkstock; ©Lorraine Kourafas/Shutterstock; ©Chamille White/Shutterstock **145** ©Jupiterimages/Thinkstock

Text credits

The authors and publishers acknowledge the following sources of copyright material and are grateful for the permissions granted. While every effort has been made, it has not always been possible to identify the sources of all the material used, or to trace all copyright holders. If any omissions are brought to our notice, we will be happy to include the appropriate acknowledgments on reprinting.

8 Text adapted from "Blind Chef Christine Ha Crowned 'MasterChef' in Finale" by Ryan Owens and Meredith Frost, *ABC News*, September 11, 2012. Reproduced with permission of ABC News.
40 Quotes from *Quiet: The Power of Introverts in a World That Can't Stop Talking* by Susan Cain, Penguin Books, 2012. Copyright ©Susan Cain. Reproduced by permission of Penguin Books Ltd.